ROUTLEDGE LIBRARY EDITIONS:
COLONIALISM AND IMPERIALISM

Volume 36

LOCAL GOVERNMENT IN WEST AFRICA

LOCAL GOVERNMENT IN WEST AFRICA

RONALD WRAITH

LONDON AND NEW YORK

First published in 1964 by George Allen & Unwin Ltd

This edition first published in 2023
by Routledge
4 Park Square, Milton Park, Abingdon, Oxon OX14 4RN

and by Routledge
605 Third Avenue, New York, NY 10158

Routledge is an imprint of the Taylor & Francis Group, an informa business

© 1964 George Allen & Unwin Ltd

All rights reserved. No part of this book may be reprinted or reproduced or utilised in any form or by any electronic, mechanical, or other means, now known or hereafter invented, including photocopying and recording, or in any information storage or retrieval system, without permission in writing from the publishers.

Trademark notice: Product or corporate names may be trademarks or registered trademarks, and are used only for identification and explanation without intent to infringe.

British Library Cataloguing in Publication Data
A catalogue record for this book is available from the British Library

ISBN: 978-1-032-41054-8 (Set)
ISBN: 978-1-032-42500-9 (Volume 36) (hbk)
ISBN: 978-1-032-42502-3 (Volume 36) (pbk)
ISBN: 978-1-003-36306-4 (Volume 36) (ebk)

DOI: 10.4324/9781003363064

Publisher's Note
The publisher has gone to great lengths to ensure the quality of this reprint but points out that some imperfections in the original copies may be apparent.

Disclaimer
The publisher has made every effort to trace copyright holders and would welcome correspondence from those they have been unable to trace.

Local Government in West Africa

BY

RONALD WRAITH, C.B.E.
University of Ibadan

London
GEORGE ALLEN AND UNWIN LTD.
RUSKIN HOUSE   MUSEUM STREET

FIRST PUBLISHED IN 1964

This book is copyright under the Berne Convention. Apart from any fair dealing for the purposes of private study, research, criticism or review, as permitted under the Copyright Act 1956, no portion may be reproduced by any process without written permission. Enquiry should be made to the publisher.

© *George Allen & Unwin Ltd*, 1964

PRINTED IN GREAT BRITAIN
in 10 *point Times Roman type*
BY C. TINLING AND CO. LTD
LIVERPOOL, LONDON AND PRESCOT

EXPLANATORY NOTE

THIS book is about local government in English-speaking West Africa, or to be precise in Nigeria, Ghana and Sierra Leone. Its arrangement presents a difficulty, because there is so much variety of practice in these areas that generalizations are impossible. A compromise has been attempted whereby the main part of the book is based on Eastern and Western Nigeria and Ghana, which have certain characteristics in common; separate chapters are then written about Northern Nigeria and Sierra Leone, where matters have taken a different course. The discussion of general local government principles, however, in Chapters 1 to 9, is relevant to all the countries alike.

A minor difficulty arises over the use of the words Ordinance, Act and Law, which may sometimes seem to be used indiscriminately. 'Ordinance' was the word used for an act of the legislature before independence; in Ghana, Sierra Leone and the *Federation* of Nigeria it has been replaced by 'Act', but in the *Regions* of Nigeria it has been replaced by 'Law'. It has not always been possible to use these words consistently.

It will make it easier to follow the argument if it is remembered that a 'region' in Ghana is roughly equivalent to a 'province' in Nigeria and Sierra Leone.

Finally, the phrase 'West Africa' invariably means 'English-speaking West Africa'.

CONTENTS

1. *Definitions* — 9
2. *The Local Authorities* — 15
3. *The Local Councils* — 25
4. *Local Government Staff* — 41
5. *Party Politics* — 57
6. *The Work of Local Authorities* — 67
7. *The Size and Population of Local Authorities* — 81
8. *Local Authorities and the Central Government* — 96
9. *The Revenue of Local Authorities* — 108
10. *Northern Nigeria* — 125
11. *Sierra Leone* — 145
12. *Some Questions for the Future* — 163

CHAPTER 1

Definitions

It is not easy to say what local government is, because it means different things in different countries.

In Britain it occupies a more important place in public administration than it does in many other countries. One reason for this is historical; when Britain was developing rapidly in the nineteenth century the function of the Government was far more restricted than it is today. It was concerned with national and international affairs, but not very much with local ones. It mostly looked after such things as foreign relations, trade, defence, taxation and law and order. The Ministries, which were much fewer than they are today, were not executive bodies, as they are now, with departments whose tentacles reach out into every town and village. Consequently, when the need for local social services grew, there were no paternal government departments which could deal with the overwhelming demand for sanitation, pure water supplies, public health, education, the care of the poor and the large variety of amenities that were needed in the new towns. When these became urgently necessary the Government therefore passed laws about them, and provided money in the form of grant aid, but it passed on the responsibility for administering them to locally elected councils of ordinary citizens.

This fitted in with the second reason, which could be called 'temperamental'; that is to say, the British on the whole do not like being governed, but since they must be governed they like as much of their government as possible to be local. There is a saying that 'he governs best who governs least', which reflects this attitude of mind. For these and other reasons 'local authorities', as the locally elected councils are called, grew to have great influence in the administration of the country and to exercise a large measure of independence in local affairs. In the last twenty-five years, as the social services they administered have become more complicated and expensive, and as great technical strides have been made which make it more efficient and economical to provide them over larger areas, this independence has greatly declined, and central and local government are more closely meshed than they used to be. But a strong tradition of independent local government was started, and the spirit still persists.

When a new kind of local administration was needed to replace the old 'native authorities' in West Africa in the early 1950's this British idea of local government was adopted, and many of its outward forms were followed, especially in Eastern and Western Nigeria and the Gold Coast (as it then was). It is not easy, in fact it is almost impossible, for one country to adopt the political institutions of another, because such institutions depend on a number of factors, which again we may call historical and temperamental, which vary among the different races and nations of the world. In the case of local government in West Africa this is shown by the fact that in the last ten years it has departed very considerably from the British model which it originally started to copy. The local government systems of Eastern and Western Nigeria and Ghana now differ greatly from the British system, and also from each other; nevertheless they all show sufficient traces of their common ancestry to make it possible to write about them together.

But if we want to understand how a political institution—like local government—works, it is helpful to compare it with how the same institution works in other countries, and to bear in mind that there are no 'rules' in these matters, but simply general principles which will always be applied differently by different people.

Local government in Britain may be defined as local

democracy, exercised through locally elected councils, whose main purpose is to provide or administer social services, with as great a degree of independence as modern circumstances allow. But we have only to look back to the West African native authorities of the 1940's to see that local government can have a quite different meaning. In those days, in Southern Nigeria and the Gold Coast, there were hundreds of small 'native authorities' which were very varied in their size and composition. In the Gold Coast and Western Nigeria they usually centred round a traditional Chief, and in Eastern Nigeria round a 'town', or clan, or some unit of local loyalty which was not always very clearly defined. They were not democratic, as we normally use the word today, but they were 'representative' in that they expressed the voice of the local people, as distinct from the colonial administrators, in local affairs. In a very small way they performed some of the duties which we now associated with local government, but their main interest and activity lay in administering justice through the native courts, rather than in administering social services for the material welfare of the people. The real local *authority* did not rest with them, but with civil servants known as Residents and District Officers (or in the Gold Coast Provincial and District Commissioners). These men represented a quite different idea of 'local government', that is an arm or extension of the central government.[1] This idea of local government is just as valid as the one usually accepted in Britain, and it is not by any means confined to a 'colonial' situation; indeed, it is the one which is normally accepted in France, and in varying degrees in other countries of continental Europe. Democracy in local government is by no means absent in France, but it is not dominant, as it is in Britain. The local councils (*conseils municipals*) have indeed important powers and duties, exercised through their principal officer the Mayor; but their proceedings are subject to the approval, direction or veto of a civil servant

[1] The first idea may be described as the 'devolution', the second as the 'decentralisation', of government functions.

(the *Prefect*) who is the 'local arm of central government', and to whom there is no corresponding figure in the British system. A rough parallel may be drawn between the Prefect and the Resident on the one hand, and the *conseil municipal* and the native authority on the other; which means that in colonial days the British administrators were operating a system of local government which more resembled the French than the British.

Although local government may mean, at the one extreme, local democracy exercised through elected councils, and at the other extreme the local administration of the central government, there are many kinds of compromise between these two extremes. Indeed, such compromises exist both in Britain and France; local autonomy in Britain is modified by an increasing amount of central control, and prefectorial government in France is subject to the democratic influence of the *conseils municipals*. There are other variations on the theme. In the United States, for example, a dozen different patterns of local government may be found, varying from east to west of the Continent and from rural to urban areas. The government of big cities is carried on variously by elected Boards of Commissioners, who after election become administrators in their own right, by 'political bosses' who exercise great personal authority, or by 'City Managers', who are professional administrators hired by the elected city councils to run the affairs of the city with a high degree of independence. The last variation is particularly interesting as it brings to local government the approach of 'big business'; that is to say the city manager and the city council have some resemblance to the managing director and the board of directors of a large firm.

This is not the place to discuss comparative local government in all its immense variety, but certain things need to be emphasized in this opening chapter, and the few facts that we have mentioned may help to draw attention to them. First, that local government in West Africa today derives from a foreign system which heavily overlays the indigenous one; secondly, that it is only one of many systems which could have been chosen if the stimulus of a foreign system was needed; and thirdly that more than most systems of local government this particular one is rooted in the history and temperament of the country of its birth.

The British system makes very heavy demands of a kind which cannot always be met in the developing countries of West Africa. In the first place, since its aim is to spread responsibility as widely as possible among the elected representatives, it makes great demands on *councillors*. Their time is much occupied, often in working hours, with large numbers of committees and sub-committees, and they are always at the disposal of the voters who elected them. Since they are not paid for what they do (indeed until 1948 they did not even receive their out-of-pocket expenses) they need to be men and women who can afford the time, which means that they must generally be people of some independence and status. Outside the cities of West Africa such people are not easy to find. Secondly, because the local authorities have so much to do which in other countries is done by the state they have to employ very large *staffs* of professional men, such as accountants, engineers and medical officers, as well as large numbers of skilled technicians and artisans; in West Africa talent of this kind is largely confined to central departments, and even there is often very thinly spread. Lastly, and again because their work is so comprehensive and varied, the *structure* of British local authorities is very complicated, there being six or seven different kinds of authority, two or even three of which may be responsible for providing different social services in the same place; to introduce such a complicated system into a country where it has not grown up naturally can cause great confusion and friction.

The points which have been briefly mentioned in the previous paragraph will recur in later chapters, but they have been mentioned now as a reminder that when we are discussing how local government works we are to a large extent discussing how a *foreign* system of local government works, and how it is adapting itself to its new environment.

This means that everything is constantly changing; the principal laws which define the powers and duties of local authorities, and their relationship to the central government, change from time to time; the rules and instructions which say, for example, how local rates are to be levied, or how the staff is to be engaged, change from year to year. It is therefore difficult to write anything about how local government works which may not be out of date before the written word is printed.

It is possible nowadays to buy useful instruction books telling us how a motor-car engine works, or how to do household repairs. These books can go on being read year after year because the things they are describing do not change, or at most they only change in minor details as people think of better ways of applying a fixed principle. This cannot be an instruction book in the same way, because what it is describing is a human institution in a rapidly changing and developing society, and even some of the main principles gradually alter, and differences of degree may become so great that they slowly develop into differences in kind.

We shall try to show how local government was *intended* to work according to its British origins, and how it has gradually come to work in a different way in its West African environment.

CHAPTER 2

The Local Authorities

By 'local authorities' we mean the corporate bodies which are set up by statute to discharge certain duties and exercise certain powers; thus the Lagos town council is a local authority. 'Local councils', which are discussed in the next chapter, mean very nearly the same thing, since legal authority is vested in the elected councillors; but it is worth preserving the distinction, so that in this chapter we can discuss the *institutions* of local government, and in the next the *people* who operate these institutions.

Local authorities in West Africa are created by Acts of Parliament, though Parliament itself does not specify exactly what these authorities shall be or what powers they shall exercise; it passes on this duty to the Minister of Local Government, who exercises what are called powers of 'delegated legislation' and sets up each separate local authority by 'Instrument'. In Britain, and consequently in West Africa, there are several kinds of local authority, in contrast to France where there is only one kind (the *commune*). In Britain they are known by the names of county borough, county, municipal borough, urban or rural district and parish; in West Africa they have been known by various names over the last few years, but are now called county and local council areas in Eastern Nigeria; divisional, district and local council areas in Western Nigeria; and urban and local council areas in Ghana; in addition all three countries make a further distinction over their most important towns, some, though not all, of which are known as 'municipalities', and in the case of Ghana 'cities'. It is best to leave these larger towns out of our reckoning for the moment, both in Britain and West Africa, and to return to them at the end of the chapter.

What remains is a pattern of local authorities in which more than one local authority operates on the same ground, though each one is responsible for doing different things. In Britain and Western Nigeria three different authorities do this; in Eastern Nigeria two; and in Ghana only one. Thus in Western Nigeria there are authorities covering a relatively large area, known as divisional councils; inside each division are several district councils; and inside each district several local councils. Eastern Nigeria, on the other hand, is divided into county councils, of only medium size, and inside each county area there are a number of local councils. In the west there are three levels and in the east two, and an English expression has been borrowed to describe them—they are sometimes called 'three-tier' and 'two-tier' systems of local government. Although the smaller authorities are contained within the boundaries of the larger ones they are not subordinate to them, but simply do different things.

This is the first point at which West African practice diverges from British. In Britain, Acts of Parliament have created local authorities with different names, and have given them different things to do; but the pattern over the country is uniform, that is to say *all* county councils and *all* rural district councils have the same powers and duties as each other. In West Africa Parliaments have created local authorities of different types but have not defined the powers and duties of each type; instead, the laws have specified a long list of powers and duties that are within the field of local government as a whole, and left it to the Minister to allocate whatever seemed appropriate to any type of council in the light of local circumstances. This has been done in the Instrument which was mentioned earlier. Thus the powers of one divisional council might differ slightly from another, or district councils might have relatively stronger or weaker powers in different parts of a region. This is a more flexible arrangement than the British one and has certain advantages.

Several criticisms may be made of the local authorities and the way they do their work, and we shall make them in later chapters; but it is important to assert at the outset that local government does in fact play a very important part in the administration of Southern Nigeria and Ghana. In a recent year in Eastern Nigeria, for example, the approved estimates for expenditure (in round figures) by all local authorities was over £4¼ million; £2¼ million of this was represented by recurrent grant from the regional government, but over £2 million was raised by the local authorities themselves through local rates. Over £1¼ million was spent by them on education, nearly £1¼ million on public works, £700,000 on local health services and £140,000 on markets. The spending of £4¼ million of public money through the channel of local government, in a country whose total recurrent budget in that year was about £20 million, is a significant fact. One-tenth of the ordinary expenditure of the Government was disbursed in this way and the local authorities added nearly the same sum themselves. In Western Nigeria the local authorities were budgeting in 1959-60 for an estimated revenue of £7·9 million, of which £4·1 million was to come from local rates, £1·3 million from government grants and £2·5 million from other sources. An even more significant figure from Western Nigeria, which shows the *growing* importance of local government, is that expenditure by local authorities rose from £1,976,861 in *1952* to £8,417,446 in *1962*.

Furthermore, all this has been achieved at a time when the local authorities were going through many 'teething troubles', were being constantly reorganized, and were suffering from corruption, shortage of staff, and consequent inefficiency. In spite of many weaknesses they represent an important, and growing, element in the administration of these countries.

Having said this, however, the question arises whether

such a large number of local authorities is needed in the circumstances of West Africa. It also arises in Britain, where there has been a controversy for many years on such matters as whether the three-tier system should be reduced to two, or whether the country should be divided into local authorities which all more or less resembled each other and exercised similar powers. But in West Africa the problem is more urgent, because it has often seemed as if there were too many local authorities, that they were all too small, and that they all had too little to do. In Eastern Nigeria and Ghana this problem has in fact been faced and the number reduced. In the former, until 1958, there were seventeen 'upper-tier' councils, known as counties, about 100 'middle-tier', known as districts, and a very much larger number of 'lower-tier', known as local council areas; in that year the seventeen counties were abolished, and the needs of the region are now virtually served by 107 districts (though to make matters more confusing the name 'county' was revived in 1961 and again substituted for 'district'). In Ghana, before 1961, there were twenty-six upper-tier and 252 lower-tier authorities, some urban but mostly rural. In that year the upper-tier authorities were abolished and the country is now served (outside the big towns) by sixty-nine councils only. In other words, there was a strikingly similar development in the two countries, and it is worth considering the reasons which brought this about.

In the first place the councils had been established, in the years 1950 (Eastern Nigeria) and 1951 (Ghana) in a considerable hurry, under political pressure, and without sufficient attention being given to the best size for them to be in relation to the work they had to do; there was a temptation in both countries to rush them into being as direct successors to the former native authorities, one of whose faults was that they were too small for efficient administration. Of the 252 lower councils in Ghana, for example, thirty-one had populations of under 5,000, the smallest being less than 1,000; and another seventy-five had populations of between 5,000 and 10,000.[1] Authorities of this size may well have served the simple needs of the old Gold Coast 'states' or Ibo 'clans', which, as we have said, were judicial as much as administrative, but they were not nearly large enough for modern local authorities whose main task is supposed to be providing their inhabitants with expensive social services.

Secondly, insufficient thought was given to the work they had to do in relation to their ability to do it. If we look at the various Acts and see what this work is, it looks impressive enough on paper. For example, the Ghana Act lists 108 distinct functions that a local authority may perform, and the Eastern Nigeria Act ninety-one, in addition to the power to make by-laws on a very wide variety of subjects. These functions vary from important ones like building hospitals, schools and water supplies; to less ambitious ones like maintaining markets, slaughter houses or recreation grounds; and to some minor ones like impounding stray animals, restricting hawkers and beggars, or even granting sums of money for the maintenance of twins. The potential work of local authorities seems to be almost as comprehensive as in Britain; but if we examine these lists more carefully, in relation to the revenue and staffs of the authorities, we see that a number of the more important ones are quite impossible in practice for the councils to perform, because they require money, technical staff and machinery which are far beyond their resources, and that the only people who can do these satisfactorily are the central departments of government; while many of the less important ones are either very local in their application or are really quite trivial. Consequently, apart from education,[2] the basic work of the authorities lies in what might be

---

[1] Report of the Commissioner for Local Government Enquiries, Accra, 1957.

[2] Education is the biggest single item of expenditure, but it must be treated separately in another chapter, as the responsibilities of the central and local authorities vary a good deal. Some schools are maintained by local authorities, some by central government, and some by both in varying degrees of partnership.

called the 'lower middle' ranges—markets, slaughter houses, dispensaries, rural water supplies, lorry parks, maintenance of minor roads, sanitary services, etc. These are very important functions, and it is not intended to belittle them; but they are not in themselves sufficient to maintain an elaborate two- or three-tier structure of local authorities, even the largest of which is probably too small to tackle anything more ambitious. If the authorities *were* very much larger the situation might be different, but in practice it is difficult to persuade people to combine together in larger units; indeed, their constant tendency is to want to break up into even smaller ones. This is a point to which are shall return in a later chapter.

The Eastern Nigeria and Ghana Governments, then, have considerably improved on the first local government legislation, but whether they have yet gone far *enough* is debatable. In Eastern Nigeria the revenue of the county councils varies from £7,000 to £90,000, the average being possibly about £40,000. In Ghana, as a result of the much more drastic reduction in the number of councils from 278 to 69, they are bigger and more viable; a number of their estimates taken at random now show revenues ranging from £51,000 to £142,000—though even these figures are not large compared with, say, the corresponding district councils in Kenya. £40,000 may seem quite a large sum of money to most of us, but for the revenue of a modern local authority it is really quite small. We will discuss this more fully later on, but here it is worth pointing out that when the overhead expenses have been met—that is the cost of the councillors' expenses, the secretary's office, the treasurer's staff, the wages of the labourers—there is comparatively little left to employ the skilled technical staff or to buy the machinery and equipment which are necessary for development.

In Western Nigeria the original three-tier system of divisional, district and local councils has not yet been altered by statute, but exactly the same problems have been experienced as in Ghana and Eastern Nigeria, and the tendency has been to reorganize in such a way that one of the three kinds of council is eliminated, either by abolishing the divisional council or by allowing local councils to fade away for lack of funds. This has not been done systematically, and the pattern of authorities now varies a good deal in different parts of the region.

But the work of modern local authorities is always much more important and urgent in towns than in rural areas, and it is a pity in many ways that so much attention has been paid in West Africa to establishing a uniform pattern of local government over the whole country, which is almost entirely rural, instead of concentrating on the towns, and working outwards from them; this has been the pattern of development in other countries, and it is the natural one.

We do not suggest that townspeople are more important than farmers, but simply that their local government problems are more difficult to solve, more urgent and of course more expensive. Although the work of local government can be very varied, its 'hard core' is sanitation and public health, which can mean such diverse things as pure water supplies, drains and sewers, the maintenance, lighting and cleaning of streets, hygienic markets and slaughter houses, refuse disposal, the prevention of disease, and in a wider sense the clearing away of slums and insanitary quarters, and replanning and building. One can see at a glance that some of this does not apply to a rural area, and that none of it is so urgent there. It is of course *desirable* that there should be similar provision in villages, but life would not come to an end if there were not, since there is space, water, fresh air and room to expand; but life might quite literally come to an end in a big town if there were not elaborate provision for getting rid of refuse, nightsoil, waste water and dirt; for bringing drinking water from distant places and purifying it; and for keeping streets, houses and public places in a hygienic condition. If these things were neglected mass disease would quickly take its toll of lives. The social problems of the towns are also greater—there is more crime, homelessness, prostitution, poverty, even hunger, since every mouthful of food must be paid for instead of being grown—and local government is concerned with some of these. There is also a growing—and alarming—problem of traffic control and public transport, and of town-planning.

The urban problems of *English-speaking* West Africa are especially acute, for it was an undoubted fault of British colonial administration that it was less interested in the developing cities than in the welfare and good government of the family farmer in the rural areas. Leaving aside their respective merits as 'colonialists', the French, the Germans and the Belgians made a better job of the cities of Africa than did the British, and the characteristics of many Nigerian and Ghanaian towns today are squalor, overcrowding, lack of planning and absence of civic dignity and pride—quite apart from the fact that their sanitary and social services are grossly inadequate.

It is all the more regrettable that representative local government was not more vigorously developed in the towns, because it was there that the most able, intelligent and experienced men could have been found as councillors—men who could have understood and assisted the work of local government, and might have set a higher standard than we know today if they had been given earlier responsibility. Town councils were of course established long ago along the west coast, in Freetown in 1893, in Accra, Sekondi and Cape Coast in 1894; but Lagos did not become a 'township' until 1919 or a municipality until 1953; and Ibadan, the largest indigenous city on the continent of Africa outside Egypt, was administered as part of a large rural area, and by a largely traditional council, until 1961. In most of the growing towns of Nigeria the 'local authority' was until very recent times an individual—an administrative officer who was in charge of the town and was assisted by an advisory board. Even today the town council of Lagos is a relatively minor authority in the sense that far more of the duties involved in governing Lagos are performed by the Federal Government and by two statutory bodies, the

Port Authority and the Lagos Executive Development Board, than by the elected council, which is primarily a sanitary authority, though it has recently taken over primary education from the Government and has acquired a bus service from private enterprise.

It is always easy to criticize, and in fairness to past administrators it must be pointed out that the early attempts at municipal government, in Sierra Leone and the Gold Coast, frequently failed through the apathy of the people —voters, councillors and staff alike—their refusal to accept the discipline of rates and their general inefficiency. Nevertheless, in the more modern era of the 1950's and 1960's too little attention has been given to modernizing local government in the big towns, which after all are the 'growing points' of any developing country; and too much has been given to imposing a uniform system of local government in the rural areas, to replace the old native authorities.

It may be convenient at this point to clear up some of the confusion which exists over names. People in West Africa often get confused over the use of such words as city, town, borough, urban and municipal; in Britain, where they originated, these words are not always very precisely used, and it is natural that Africans should find it difficult to sort them out, especially when peculiar English expressions like 'county borough', 'municipal borough' and 'urban district' are brought into discussion. There is no significant difference between a city and a town; in Britain greater prestige attaches to the former and it is usually thought of as being a bigger or more important place, but it is a ceremonial rather than a practical difference. Borough is simply an ancient name for a town. The adjective 'municipal' means, in its literal sense, anything concerned with local government, but is commonly used to denote the government of towns, as distinct from rural areas. The names given to particular kinds of local authority in Britain—county borough, municipal or non-county borough and urban district —need not detain the West African reader for more than a moment, as they have no relevance whatever to his own country. A county borough is, in the administrative sense, the most powerful of all local authorities, as it exercises *all* the powers that any local authority may by law exercise within its own boundaries; there are no towns in West Africa with functions nearly as comprehensive as this. Leaving the county boroughs aside, municipal or non-county boroughs are the older and on the whole larger towns, and urban districts the newer and smaller ones.

In considering local government in West Africa it is wise to forget these British names, and it is unprofitable to try to draw parallels with West African local authorities. The names only arise at all because in the early 1950's a great deal of British nomenclature was imported into Nigeria and Ghana, and some of it, rather inappropriately, survives. But this is just an accident of history, and throws no light whatever on the real nature of the problems.

What is much more important is to remember that the closer people live together, and the larger the groups in which they live, the more practical problems have to be tackled in the sphere of local government. This gives urban local government its special importance. The provision of these social services is not the *only* justification for local government, but it is the principal one, and without it local authorities would be scarcely worth having. In rural areas these needs are less urgent and less demanding. If both urban and rural needs could be tackled simultaneously, so much the better; but if it is a question of priorities—and in developing countries nearly everything turns out to be a question of priorities—good urban local government is immeasurably more important.

CHAPTER 3

The Local Councils

A COUNCIL, to use a customary legal description, is a 'body corporate having perpetual succession and a common seal and having the power to sue and to be sued'. This means that the council is the local *authority*, upon which the Government lays certain powers and duties, which may tax people for local purposes, and which must accept responsibility for good government in such matters as are within its competence; it may also be disciplined by the higher authority of the Government if it misbehaves itself or is grossly negligent or inefficient. But the council consists of ordinary men and women elected by adult suffrage for a period of three years, and although their responsibility is corporate none of them can escape a measure of individual responsibility; each will discover this if he is, for example, a party to the misuse of the council's funds, since he may be 'surcharged', i.e. made to pay back from his own pocket his share of the money which has been misused.

Councillors, then, are always important people. British practice increases their importance by requiring them to meet frequently, to serve on many committees and sub-committees, and by giving them real, as distinct from nominal, responsibility in making plans and decisions. The staffs of local authorities, the local civil services so to speak, will carry on the routine business of the council without troubling the councillors; and principal officers may even make quite important decisions on their own authority; the extent to which they do this will depend very largely on personal relations and on local custom; but no principal officer will make a decision which involves a question of policy or principle, or the expenditure of public money, himself, but will always ask his committee for instructions. The ordinary councillor spends many hours a week on his work, and the chairman of a committee, particularly in a large authority, may find himself with practically a full-time job; for which, however, he is not paid anything.

It is not necessary for councillors to be worked so hard, or to have so much responsibility put upon them, or indeed to have so many councillors or so many committees. Local government in several other countries, although having a 'conciliar' system, asks far less of councillors and gives more responsibility to permanent officials; meetings are less frequent, committees are very much fewer and councils go into far less detail; even in neighbouring Eire this is so, for the local authorities there employ officials called 'managers', who, as their name implies, administer the affairs of the authority with a much freer hand than their British counterparts.

However, West Africa chose, rightly or wrongly, to follow British practice in this matter, and although many things have changed since the early 1950's this particular aspect of local government has not.

It may as well be said bluntly, and at this early stage, that the quality and performance of councillors in West Africa has been deeply disappointing. The system which was copied from Britain makes certain assumptions about councillors which it would be impossible to put into the law, but which are nevertheless more important than anything which *is* in the law; that is to say, the law governing this kind of local government can never work satisfactorily unless these assumptions are well founded.

One is that the men and women who offer themselves for election to local councils are people of some standing and reputation in their neighbourhood; from which it usually follows that they have established themselves in their own job or profession and do not stand for election with any idea of material profit for themselves. Another is that they are people of sufficient education or intelligence to be able to look at the problems of public welfare dispassionately, and to make decisions based on what they honestly think is best for the local community. Another is that whatever mixed motives may have caused them to become councillors, a dominant motive is that of public service. Another is that they are ordinarily honest.

There are some disadvantages in expecting these standards, the chief of which is that if councillors are to be people of some local standing and reputation they tend to be rather elderly, and it is generally thought that as people get older they become more conservative and less progressive. This tendency to be elderly is increased by the great demands that local government makes on councillors' time, since it is often only people who have retired, or are wealthy, or who are in the fortunate position of being their own masters, who can spare the necessary amount of time away from the job of earning their own living. This is particularly true of rural or scattered areas, where they have to travel some distance to attend meetings; it is less true in towns, where meetings are usually held in the evenings, after working hours.

But if assumptions of this kind are not made local government may become valueless, or even dangerous.

This raises the whole question of the remuneration of councillors, and since there is no more thorny question in local government in West Africa it will be as well to deal with it now, before going on to discuss the normal duties of a councillor.

The first thing to be said is that the question of paying certain councillors is one that has been discussed for some time in Britain and which may shortly have to be faced.[1] There is no question of *all* councillors in *all* kinds of councils being paid, for this would be unnecessary, in-

[1] Mayors of boroughs are normally given 'salaries' to enable them to perform their public and ceremonial duties, but this is not regarded as personal remuneration, and may well result in loss.

tolerably expensive, and against public sentiment. Two things have happened, however, within recent years which makes the position of some leading councillors in the larger authorities (the county boroughs and the larger counties) increasingly burdensome. The first is that although these authorities have been losing some of their powers because some of their former functions have been 'nationalized', the total volume of their work has continued to grow, and they are now involved in vast development plans for education, health, public works and planning; the second is that social conditions have changed, in that there are fewer wealthy or leisured people than there use to be, and business and professional men have to give more and more time to their own occupations, and can no longer spare so much for public service. The burden on all councillors is considerable, but for those who are, for example, chairmen of important committees in the big authorities it is becoming intolerable. At some time in the near future local government may either have to pay such men or lose their services. The ordinary councillor is not in this position, but even so he is often not as fortunate as his predecessors in the early part of the century; moreover it is no longer acceptable to public opinion that service on councils should be the privilege of the few who, for whatever reason, are able to spare the time and the money, and local government is richer for the presence on its councils of ordinary wage-earners and housewives. It is interesting that less than twenty years ago there was no general code which allowed councillors even to claim their travelling or out-of-pocket expenses. Not until the Local Government Act of 1948 was this put on a systematic basis. This Act also authorized, for the first time, payments to councillors to cover proved loss of earnings, though the great majority of councillors do not take advantage of this because their earnings cannot be shown to have diminished directly, though they may well have done so indirectly, as a result of their local government duties. All this reflects the fact that membership of local councils was normally regarded as a duty, a public service or a hobby, and the concessions that have been made are not intended to alter this principle.

But whereas in Britain the question of councillors' expenses was not dealt with for fifty years, and the actual payment of councillors has not even now been considered, in West Africa it has been a dominant consideration since the native authorities were first reorganized, and an extraordinary amount of public time has been consumed in discussing 'sitting allowances' (which are universally paid) and other forms of remuneration; while today there is a considerable demand for the actual payment of salaries. It would be wrong to criticize this solely in the light of British practice, for any such comparison would be superficial and misleading. The much more fundamental point is that councillors in the two countries are wholly different kinds of people; in other words, the 'assumptions' that we made a little earlier do not in fact apply in West Africa.

Generally speaking, men who stand for local councils are not successful or established men; they are often very young, which is understandable since most of the older generation outside the towns would probably be illiterate; many of them are teachers, earning very small salaries; others have no definable occupation, and regard their council membership as a way of supplementing, if not actually earning, a living. A high proportion are neither intelligent nor honest, and it is these who deter more reputable citizens from standing for local councils. Above all, local councils have virtually become appendages of the political parties and the first qualification for a councillor is to be a political 'activist'. The dishonesty of councils has come to be taken for granted, a fact which can be stated openly since it is the subject of so many official reports. No one seriously questions the fact that the chief purpose of many—indeed most—councillors is to enrich themselves by percentages on contracts, bribes for favours and corrupt practice in general; or that nepotism, the giving of jobs, market stalls or contracts to relatives, is common practice.

All this is so familiar to West African readers that there

is no point in dwelling on it. It is more profitable to point out that it constitutes a perversion, not an adaptation, of the British type of local government which was chosen in preference to any other. The system assumes conditions which do not exist in West Africa today. The questions which arise, constructively, are whether the position can be improved without the system being virtually destroyed; and what are, normally, the duties and responsibilities of councillors in this conciliar type of local government?

With regard to the first question, there has already been some improvement, and small though this may have been in relation to the problem as a whole it suggests that things are moving forward and not backward. It must be confessed that much of the improvement has been due to negative, or punitive, measures designed to prevent councillors from being corrupt and irresponsible. Thus it is now fairly common practice for 'the Minister', which in practice means a local administrative officer, to control the award of all contracts over a relatively small amount, to make or at least ratify all appointments to the staff above a certain level, and of course to scrutinize and approve a council's annual estimates. Moreover, the power of 'surcharge', that is the right of the Government to recover from individual councillors sums that have been improperly disbursed, is being more frequently used, specially in the Eastern Region of Nigeria; and this has had a salutary effect, as it makes councillors realize both that their responsibilities are serious and that the Government 'means business'.

Evidence of a more positive kind of improvement, arising from a growing sense of public service, is more difficult to give. All that can be given in fact is the hearsay evidence of people whose work is concerned with the local authorities and who have seen them at work over a number of years. What they have to say is sometimes mildly encouraging, at other times pessimistic. It can be said as a fact that expenditure by and through local authorities has grown steadily in the ten years between the early 1950's and the early 1960's, that despite many amendments to the law the main fabric of the new local government has been preserved, and that without the work of the local authorities the central departments of government would be intolerably hard pressed. But at the personal level—and we are discussing councillors, the living embodiment of local government—there is only occasional evidence that a higher calibre of man is seeking election, that a spirit of public service is growing or that bribery, corruption and nepotism are declining.

The reasons for this are complex, and beyond the scope of this book, but the principal ones must just be mentioned, even if there is no space to elaborate them. First, local government is an alien institution which does not yet command much loyalty; men who are completely honest in their dealings with family, clan and tribe or any indigenous institution are often dishonest in their dealings as councillors. Second, the total number of people available in West Africa of the kind which the British type of local government takes for granted is small; such as they are, they are much more drawn to national politics or to their professions and businesses than to the rather trivial and often sordid affairs of local councils. Third, and arising from the second, the majority of people engaging in rural local government must necessarily, at this stage, be illiterate, and it is not easy for men of higher calibre to work alongside them; in any case such men usually gravitate to the towns. Fourth, the council areas are small in population and revenue, and the volume and importance of the business each is able to handle is such that men of standing are not interested in it. Fifth, as we have said, the councils are so deeply embroiled in politics that busy people with businesses or professions of their own cannot be bothered with them; or alternatively if they have political interests they are in national, not local, politics. Of these five factors only the fourth, and possibly the fifth, could be improved by Government action in the forseeable future; they are the subject of later chapters.

None of these considerations ought to apply in the large towns, where the work of the councils is sufficiently challenging to tax the powers of the most able, where the revenues, though inadequate, are at least sufficient to bring about visible improvements, and where there is a sufficient concentration of educated and established citizens to satisfy the demands of the British type of local government. It must be confessed, however, that their record is no better than that of the rural councils; in Nigeria alone, all the major urban authorities, Lagos, Abeokuta, Ibadan, Kano, Onitsha, Enugu, Aba and Port Harcourt have been the subject of official enquiries into maladministration and corruption, and sometimes to replacement by a 'committee of management' or a 'sole administrator'. The factors which apply in the country are also sufficiently strong in the towns.

The second question—whether the system can be sufficiently improved without destroying it—is one that can only be answered as the book proceeds. Already a number of the undoubted improvements, such as the closer control of councils by the central government, are a contradiction of the kind of local government which was first envisaged, which depends on having as much, not as little, local autonomy as possible. However, we said in the first chapter that we were studying a foreign system which was in the process of adapting itself to local circumstances, and we must not be surprised if some of these adaptations are of a radical kind.

Having considered what sort of people councillors are supposed to be, let us consider what they are supposed to do.

In the first place, they are elected to represent a small 'constituency', often called a 'ward', by direct election, and they remain in office for three years. The procedure hardly differs from that of a parliamentary election. In Western and Eastern Nigeria, not all the council members are elected, since a proportion of places may be reserved for 'traditional' members, that is chiefs and their office-bearers; this was so in Ghana also until 1961, when the Government adopted a new principle whereby chiefs were excluded from the local councils, but in compensation for this traditional councils were given new status under the

Chieftancy Act of 1961; this whole question of traditional elements in local government will be discussed later in the chapter. Occasionally, as in Western Nigeria at the time of writing, not all elections are direct; divisional councillors are elected by the constituent districts, and not by the electors. But with these exceptions the method of being elected a councillor is the same as that of being elected a Member of Parliament.

The first duty of a councillor is to represent the people who elected him, and here a curious misunderstanding often arises. So strong is local rivalry, of a quasi-political kind, that many councillors (and even some MPs) appear to think that they represent only the people who voted for them—their own supporters. If it is suggested that they equally represent the people who voted against them, provided they live in the same ward, they are surprised; if it is then asked *who* represents these people, the answer is that they have no representative because they voted for the losing candidate. This raises an important question of principle in representative democracy, and introduces the difference between a 'representative' and a 'delegate'. The theory of this kind of democracy is that a man represents all the people who live in a certain area, whether they voted for him or not, or whether they voted at all; his concern is with the total welfare of that constituency or ward. Moreover he has, in theory at any rate, the full right to speak and vote according to his own judgement, and is not tied down by what 'his people' have told him to say, or expect him to say; this happens more rarely than it used to, in Britain as elsewhere, because councillors are increasingly elected with the help of political parties, and are expected to conform to the policies of these parties; but the principle remains, and from time to time a man takes an individual and unpopular line, but nevertheless cannot be removed from his seat on the council, or in Parliament, until the next election.

Furthermore, if a man may only speak and vote in the way he has been instructed by his supporters, he is a 'delegate' or mouthpiece, and not a 'representative'. Democracy of this kind is quite legitimate, and if West Africa prefers it there is no reason to feel ashamed of it; but it is different from representative democracy, and it has the disadvantage that a man's constituents who are not also his personal supporters are virtually disfranchised.

The theory really goes a little further than this. A councillor (or MP) is supposed to think of the welfare of his local authority (or country) and not primarily of his ward (or constituency). While it is of course legitimate for him to press the interests of his own ward he should be willing to subordinate them to the interests of his council area as a whole. But this is an attitude which requires a great deal of restraint and maturity, and it is significant that there have been complaints in the West African Press that when Parliament assembles Members do little more than press the Government to provide amenities in their own constituencies.

The councillor's second duty is to attend meetings. This book is intended to promote thought and discussion, and is not a handbook for councillors, or a manual of the procedure governing meetings; accordingly little space will be given to such questions as standing orders, debating procedure, the tabling of motions or the conduct of day-to-day business. It may be doubted whether these are in any case matters of first importance at this stage; it is possible that too much emphasis has been placed upon them in the past, since in practice councils either conduct their business with great informality, or, if they attempt to follow complicated foreign rules and conventions of procedure they become so involved in them that it becomes impossible for any business to proceed at all. This is one of the many matters in which West Africans would be better advised to follow their own instincts and modes of behaviour instead of relying on British practice. Nevertheless, meetings anywhere would be chaotic if they were not governed by rules, and it is the councillor's responsibility to understand them and abide by them; they govern such matters as the order of business, how he may introduce a matter to his council, how long and how often he may speak, how subjects are brought to a conclusion, how voting takes place and how decisions are implemented. He is also expected to study his agenda papers and give some thought to the business before the meeting takes place; sometimes this is all too easy, as the agenda is brief and uninformative, but a well-prepared agenda will include a great deal of information, prepared by the council's officials, and consisting largely of the reports of committees, which set out the facts, the problems and the alternative courses of action open to the council in making its decisions. It follows from what has been said in this paragraph that the lot of the illiterate or uneducated councillor is not an easy one; indeed it is questionable whether this kind of local government should be operated at all by councillors below a certain level of education.

Under the system which has been adopted in West Africa the councils work very largely through committees, a habit for which the British are especially renowned. Some committees are compulsory, that is to say the local government law specifies that they *must* be appointed; these always include a finance committee; in Western Nigeria they include also a medical and health committee, and in Ghana committees for staff, education and development; but councils may appoint other committees, either permanently, to deal with part of their regular business, or from time to time to deal with special business. Committees other than the finance committee may co-opt members who are not councillors, up to a certain proportion; and councils may, except for financial business and the making of by-laws, delegate powers to committees; that is, the committees may make decisions and report them to the council, instead of merely making recommendations.

All this follows British local government practice very closely, and it is one of the ways in which the British system carries out its object of spreading responsibility widely among elected representatives. (Other systems of local government do without such an elaborate committee structure.) In a large council, of 40–60 members, committees are obviously essential if councillors are to have any real part in initiating and preparing business. A council cannot consider its estimates unless they have been prepared in advance; it cannot decide whether to build a school unless someone has gone into such matters as siting, design and cost; it cannot employ a member of staff unless a few people have interviewed the most likely candidates. Unless, therefore, the preparation of business is to be left to the council's permanent staff, which is the other alternative, a council's business must be very largely done in committee, and this is in fact where most of the important work is done in British local government. The power of delegation is fairly widely used in Britain, and the council, in full session, accepts or ratifies the vast majority of its committees' decisions without question, only debating particularly contentious matters of points of principle.

The system only works satisfactorily, however, if certain conventions (i.e. unwritten rules) are observed. One is that when committees are appointed they shall be representative of all points of view, and not narrowly sectional. This has not always been done in West Africa, and it is significant that in Western Nigeria a section is included in the law giving the Minister the right to require a council to appoint certain other members if he thinks that the committee in question has been 'packed'; in plain language, if the ruling party has put all its supporters on the committee and none of its opponents. Another is that the council shall not do the work of its committees all over again in full session, a temptation into which many West African councils fall; even if a committee has not been given delegated powers, and if its conclusions are therefore subject to the approval of the council, it is a waste of time and energy, and a denial of the committee system, to go over the whole ground again instead of debating and deciding the vital point.

In smaller councils doubts have often been raised as to whether so many committees are necessary. No one can answer this categorically; the answer depends on whether it is desired to spread responsibility among councillors or to concentrate it in the hands of officials; and the answer to this question may not be the same at all times and in all places.

Finally, it needs to be emphasized that a local government council is not, as is sometimes supposed, a sort of miniature parliament. In Parliament, a number of the leading members (ministers and others) are charged with important executive responsibilities, and have a staff of civil servants to carry out their policy. In a local council no councillor has any executive responsibility whatever;[1] this even applies to the mayor of a municipality; he has certain privileges and prestige as the town's chief citizen, and has certain civic duties to discharge which no other councillor can discharge; but even he is just an ordinary councillor as far as executive responsibility is concerned. It is the staff, and not the councillors, who implement the decisions made by the council; and it is the responsibility of the chief executive officer, the secretary, to see that they are implemented. The distinction between the legislative function of the councillor and the executive function of the staff has often been blurred in West Africa, with the result that councillors have interfered in the work of the secretary's office, written letters on behalf of the council, and given instructions to members of the staff. This is contrary to the intention of the local government laws and to the accepted practice of this particular type of local democracy. We shall return to the point in Chapter 5.

Traditional members of councils

The form of local government which preceded the present one was known as native administration. It lasted in Eastern Nigeria until 1950, in Ghana until 1951 and in Western Nigeria until 1952. In Ghana and Western Nigeria it was founded on the institution of chieftainship, and what we would now think of as the local council was the chief and

[1] The remarks in this paragraph do not apply to the Northern Region of Nigeria (see p. 130). See also p. 65, where the point is raised as to whether British local councils *ought* to be run on the lines of a parliament.

his traditional office bearers and advisers. No member was elected through the ballot box.

When elected councils were introduced the position of the chief was seriously affected. Was he to be superseded by the elected council? Was he to preside over it? Was his voice to count for no more than anybody else's voice? These were difficult questions. On the one hand it could be argued that the chiefs, or most of them, were old men, were illiterate, had been brought up in a tradition that was passing away, and knew little or nothing of the working of a modern institution designed to develop social services. On the other hand it could be said with equal truth that the great majority of people retained—indeed still retain—a respect for the chiefs, that they were the accepted source of authority in all customary matters, and that to leave the chief out of the government of his locality was unthinkable. Moreover, although the numerical majority of the chiefs may have been simple and illiterate men there were many outstanding exceptions; several paramount chiefs and obas were educated and progressive men with a notable record of public service in national affairs.

The problem was tackled by a compromise. Councils were to be elected, but a minority of seats was to be reserved for chiefs and other 'traditional' members, and usually the chief became the ceremonial president, as distinct from the working chairman, of the new councils. In the Western Region of Nigeria the law now reads that 'the Instrument relating to a council shall include traditional members', without specifying any maximum, which is a change from the original fixed proportion. Eastern Nigeria was not originally concerned in this matter, but as recently as 1960 their Government decided that 'all first and second class chiefs should be appointed traditional members of their respective county councils, and the Instruments of these councils were amended to provide for these appointments'.[1]

These arrangements have been much criticized, on three grounds. First, that the significance of chieftainship is largely

[1] Annual Report of the Ministry of Local Government, 1960-61.

removed if chiefs or traditional members can be outvoted by elected members, especially by young and sometimes irresponsible men; certainly the traditional members themselves have often complained of this. Second, that the traditional members are often not really interested in the modern affairs of the councils, and are a drag on the wheels because they constantly intrigue for the maintenance of their own local power and prestige. Third (in Nigeria), because governments have used their power to nominate traditional members as a device to get support for their own parties and policies.

Taken together, these criticisms carry considerable weight, and no doubt they were in the mind of the Government of Ghana when, in 1961, the Government settled the argument by taking the chiefs out of local government altogether, but regularizing their position in a Chieftaincy Act which established their own traditional councils for traditional purposes. For many years chieftaincy disputes, or quarrels between the traditional and elected elements, had laid a tremendous burden on the Ministry of Local Government, and the work involved was unrewarding and unconstructive.

Since it is difficult to argue that the purposes of local government, as set out in the Acts of Parliament, have very much to do with customary matters such as titles, customary law, inheritance or matrimonial affairs, it certainly seems logical to separate them in this way. It is admittedly difficult to generalize, because not all chiefs are alike, and local government would be infinitely better for the advice of some of the more educated and progressive of them. But taking the situation as a whole two quite separate kinds of interest seem to be involved.

However this may be, and it is of course a matter of opinion, the facts are that in Ghana the councils are now wholly elected,[1] while in Nigeria traditional members may be included in them in the Instruments by which they are established, at the discretion of the governments.

[1] The Ministry may appoint a paramount chief to be 'president' of a council, but his position is largely ceremonial.

Some Africans have observed that there is a British precedent for including a proportion of traditional members on certain councils, because of the office of 'alderman', which might roughly be translated 'elder' if not 'chief'! But the argument does not stand examination. It is true that the office of alderman is a departure from direct representative democracy, and many people in Britain criticize it on that ground; indeed, proposals are made from time to time to do away with it.

It originated in the Municipal Corporations Act of 1835, when borough councils were first elected on a systematic ratepayers' franchise and was, to put it bluntly, a concession to Conservative fears that fully elected councils would not be fit to govern properly; a sentiment with which Africans will be familiar from colonial days, and which it is interesting to find in nineteenth-century Britain. The princple, which was later extended to county councils, ensures that a quarter of the council members are elected, not by the electorate, but by the council itself, either from inside or outside its own membership; moreover such members hold office for six years instead of three. During the 130 years that have passed the real reason for its institution has tended to be forgotten, and it is now rationalized on the ground that it provides additional stability and experience, and may be used either to gain the services of some exceptionally able person, or to reward long and faithful service. It has indeed been used to good effect for both purposes, and in councils governed by party politics there has generally been some sensible agreement between the parties for the distribution of aldermanic seats. Of recent years, however, it has also been abused by political parties, who have been known to use their electoral powers, in evenly balanced councils, to maintain their own majority.

It is a debatable matter. The immediate point is that it can hardly be compared accurately with the institution of chieftainship in Africa; indeed, in the African context one can rather imagine it being quoted as a neo-colonialist device.

CHAPTER 4

Local Government Staff

ALTHOUGH responsibility for the acts and decisions of a local authority rests with the elected council, the actual work must be carried out by its paid staff. The staff are not altogether free from some personal responsibility themselves; it is their duty to advise their council and loyally to implement the council's policy; on the other hand, if they believe that any decision of the council is improper they have a right to have their opinion recorded, while if they believe it to be illegal they have a direct duty to the public and the Government to refuse to implement it. But leaving aside such unlikely possibilities it is broadly true to say that the elected councillors arrive at decisions and that the staff translate these decisions into action. How does this work in practice? Once more it will be useful to see how it works in Britain, from which the system derived, and then to see what departures from British practice have been made in recent years in response to local circumstances; they are in fact considerable.

It must first be emphasized that no realistic comparison can be drawn between the staffs of British local authorities and those in the parts of West Africa which we are discussing. The staff of a major British authority, urban or rural, will include numbers of men and women with professional and technical qualifications in the fields of engineering, medicine, public health, education, accountancy and law; and even a small urban or rural district will employ a professionally qualified secretary, treasurer, engineer, surveyor, medical officer and sanitary inspector; in Southern Nigeria and Ghana the corresponding people are in central, not local, government employment. For the most part the local authorities in West Africa are staffed by a secretary, a treasurer (though often these two posts are combined) and a works foreman or supervisor with little mechanical equipment and only a small staff of unskilled labourers; even the big cities have a staff equivalent, at most, to an English rural district council; there may also, according to local policy in this matter, be a local education officer. This situation arises partly from the different share in national administration which is borne by local authorities in the two places, partly from the small financial scale on which West African local authorities operate, and partly from the chronic shortage of qualified staff in the professional and technical ranges.

In Britain these local officials, together with their subordinate and clerical staffs, are engaged and paid by the local authorities, and are in the fullest sense their employees; if they wish to change their job, from one authority to another, they must apply for a post in answer to an advertisement, as there is no central direction in matters of this kind. Service in local government, covering a very wide range of occupations, is regarded as an honourable profession in itself, and the principal officers have a status as high as the most senior civil servants. There is, to be precise, a certain amount of central control over a few professional appointments; medical officers of health and sanitary inspectors are protected from dismissal by the Minister, and their duties and qualifications may also be prescribed by him; also chief constables and chief education officers may only be appointed with the approval of the Home Secretary or the Minister of Education; there are very good reasons for these particular controls, but they are exceptions to the general rule, and all the officials concerned are employees of the local authority, and not of the Government, even though the Government reserves the right to have a say in their appointment or dismissal.

Service in local government, then, is a profession which embraces many other professions; the wider professional interest is safeguarded through a national ssociation or trade union, the National and Local Government Officers' Association (NALGO), besides which there are many 'internal' professional associations, such as those of town clerks, municipal engineers, municipal treasurers, public health officers and so on. These are of course voluntary associations, and have nothing to do either with the central departments or the local authorities.

These local authority staffs, numbering thousands in a large authority and hundreds even in a medium-sized one, are, so to speak, the elected council's 'civil service', and enjoy the same respect and the same neutrality as the actual Civil Service. The principal officers are expected to advise the council, or more particularly the committee responsible for their own field of work, and when a committee or council decision has been made they are expected to implement it loyally, whether they agree with it or not. In practice, sharp disagreement rarely arises, because of the conventions which have grown up about the relationship of councillors and officials. It is always difficult to describe a convention, which is simply an accepted code of behaviour, though a convention may often be as important as a law. In this instance the key to the relationship is mutual respect. Constitutionally the council is the master and the official is its servant; conventionally, they work as partners in a team; what results from this is usually a workable compromise between what the expert would like and what the layman considers possible.

Since this relationship is the vital core of local government, and since it has lamentably failed to establish itself in West Africa, it is worth dwelling on it for another moment. Many West African observers in Britain have come to the conclusion that local government is a sham, because everything of any importance appears to them to be settled by the officials, who merely pull the councillors along with them. This is partly a surprised reaction from the situation in West Africa itself, where councillors tend to 'throw their weight about' and treat their officials as subordinates; and partly a misunderstanding of the relationship they observe in England. Officials who have worked for a council for a long time, and have demonstrated their efficiency and loyalty, are naturally entrusted with very large responsibilities; they are, after all, professional men, highly qualified and highly paid, and local government is their career; no sensible body of councillors will want to diminish their responsibilities or to 'cramp their style'. They are experts in their subject, they spend their whole time on it, and they know far more about it than the council. What the council, or its committees, is concerned with, is that the official shall keep in close touch with his chairman, that matters of policy shall be decided by elected representatives and not by officials, and that plans of development shall be submitted to them, with full information about the pros and cons of alternative courses, so that they may decide what is best in the interest of their fellow citizens. It must be remembered, however, that all the information and expert knowledge, as well as most of the initiative and imagination, come from the official, whose job it is to supply them; they do not come from the councillors. The job of the elected representative is to examine the officials' plans in the light of what money is available, what course of action will commend itself to the electors whom they represent, what can be done now and what must be postponed, and, occasionally, whether the professional expert in his enthusiasm is wanting to go further than public opinion will allow. The councillors, after all, are experts in one thing only—judging the wishes of the ratepayers and electors, and using their own common sense about what ought to be done.

Accordingly, if the relationship is good the councillors will give their officials a very free hand to get on with their professional job; and the officials for their part will be careful not to abuse this privilege by taking decisions about which their 'masters' might want to express an opinion. Since this mutual confidence generally exists, local government on the British pattern works; if it did not exist, it would be better to try some other system altogether. But it exists only because councillors are sensible people, and officials are competent and conscientious.

Finally, with regard to Britain, officials are completely outsde the party political battle. Like civil servants, they serve a Labour or Conservative council with equal fidelity; and no councillor would know, or would be interested in, the personal political beliefs of the council's employees. Local government employees have in fact somewhat wider freedom to take part in politics than most civil servants, but senior officials of a local authority would certainly not take advantage of this, and would confine their politics to using their vote every few years.

This is the kind of situation which the Local Government Ordinances in West Africa sought to reproduce. They failed, almost completely. Let us take the points one by one and consider why they failed, and what pattern has taken their place.

Firstly, the employment of staff by local authorities, acting as independent employers, is gradually giving way to control or even employment by the Government, thus creating a centralized or 'unified' local government service. This has been found necessary in order to protect local government staff from being victimized by irresponsible employing councils. The earlier local government Ordinances aimed at reproducing the British situation, but it was found that when councils were given this independent status as employers they frequently abused it; thus men who were performing their duties satisfactorily were dismissed because they did not belong to the right political party, or faction, or family, and were replaced by favourite sons of the party or by relatives of influential councillors. Apart from being unjust this was completely demoralizing for the staffs of local authorities everywhere, and it would have become impossible to hold anyone in local government service, let alone attract men of a higher calibre, if governments had not assumed a large measure of control. Another complication, not necessarily involving corruption, was that councils which had a free hand in the appointment of their more senior employees would frequently appoint a local man, a 'son of the soil', in preference to a better qualified man from elsewhere. It could of course be argued that, other things being equal, a son of the soil might give better service to his council than a 'stranger', but even in the best circumstances the method has its disadvantages. Firstly, sons of the soil were too deeply involved in local politics, feuds and personalities to stand any chance of being impartial; and second, it was a method which blocked that free movement from one place to another, by which senior local government officers normally gain both their experience and promotion. Accordingly, governments have, in varying degrees, stepped in both to protect and to contol the employees of local authorities.

It is a moot point whether this process of unification has gone further in Eastern or Western Nigeria; it is well advanced in both, though it has taken rather different forms.

The Eastern Ordinance of 1950 gave councils a free hand in the appointment of staff who were paid less than £400 a year; above that figure the authority of the Government was required, but in all cases the local authority could itself determine what was a reasonable remuneration for the various posts. This freedom was severely restricted in the subsequent Ordinance of 1955, which decreed that the appointment of *all* staff (even including daily-paid labourers) must be subject to the approval of the Minister, and that *no* employee was to be dismissed for any reason without the Minister's written approval; moreover the Minister assumed power to determine, if he thought fit, what was reasonable remuneration for any given post. Later the Minister did in fact lay down comprehensive regulations governing the whole field of appointments to local authority staff, including salaries, grades of employment, qualifications, procedure to be followed in making appointments, and discipline. These were long strides in the direction of central control, but an even more significant change was made in 1958, when the Minister assumed power to 'transfer an officer or member of the staff of a council to the service of another council within the Region'. Since that date many hundreds of such transfers have in fact been made, with a mixture of happy and unhappy results; happy, in that the air has been cleared, more men have been given appropriate responsibilities and have escaped from the deadening prospect of life-long employment with one small council (the curse of the 'son of the soil' policy), and corruption has been diminished; unhappy, in that the number of transfers has been excessive, to the point of having a generally unsettling effect, that men have simply moved from one set of local entanglements to another, and have as a result constantly moved from place to place. It is one thing for the Minister to decree that a man shall serve in a given place, but if local government is to mean anything at all he can only do so fruitfully if he is acceptable to a local council and if they make his path easy.

It is strange that having gone so far towards central control the Government has not taken the final step (as it has done in the Western Region) of formally establishing a unified local government service. It has stopped just short of this. There is a Local Government Service Board, but its powers are advisory and not executive; and the councils still have the power to recommend the original appointments, either as a result of advertising for candidates or by choosing someone they want to employ.

The Western Region has approached the matter a little differently. It has created a Unified Local Government Service in the formal sense, and has established a Local Government Service Board with executive, as distinct from advisory, powers. On the other hand it has not brought *all* local council employees within the scope either of the Service or the Board, but only those who are deemed to hold 'superior posts'; the definition of a superior post is made by the Governor in Council, and may be extended from time to time; currently, it includes secretaries, treasurers and local education officers, but there is continual pressure from the lower paid employees to be brought within the scope of the Unified Service so that they may enjoy greater security and status. The fortunate ones who are included are, as in the East, subject to transfer from one post to another.

The Ghana Local Government Act of 1961 reaches the same destination by a slightly different route. In principle, it leaves all councils, municipal, urban and local, free to appoint and dismiss their own staff, and thus holds to the original intention inherited from British practice. But this is subject to a vitally important qualification, contained in section 125 of the Act, which allows the Minister, *with the prior approval of the President*, to make staff regulations covering every detail of employment—qualifications, pay, promotion, discipline and 'terms and conditions of service generally'; moreover these regulations may apply to 'any class or grade of officer' in local government employment. The section also establishes a 'Local Government Central Advisory Committee' whose functions may in turn be delegated to regional committees. It thus makes possible a complete apparatus of central control over local government staff, and one moreover of which the President is the ultimate head.

Another section gives the Minister a further significant power:

'. . . a council may, with the approval of the Minister and with the consent of the officer concerned, *and shall if the Minister so directs*, appoint to any office in its service a person who is a public officer seconded to the service of the council for that purpose . . .'

In other words, administrative officers of the central government may be seconded as local government officials. The Southern Nigerian laws include a somewhat similar, but less positive, provision; there a council may appoint such an officer if the Governor or Minister approves, but the Minister does not assume the original power himself. The secondment of administrative officers to certain councils, and for particular reasons, could be a useful device, and was at one time favoured in Western Nigeria. Its obvious limitation is that there are many councils and few administrative officers, who are greatly in demand for other duties. Accordingly it could only be used in very exceptional circumstances, and Western Nigeria was never able to develop it, although it had some success.

Thus, the details differ, but the general trend is the same —a trend away from the full independence of councils in appointing staff, and towards supervision by the central authority. Whether this trend is healthy or unhealthy must remain a matter of opinion, and the fact is that the arguments are very evenly balanced. On the one hand those accustomed to the British approach would argue that independence in the appointment of staff (with the professional exceptions already referred to) is absolutely basic to the whole concept of local government; that a so-called unified local government service is simply a junior civil service, a poor relation of the proper one; that it would be more logical to 'go the whole hog' and incorporate local government officers in the real Civil Service; and that then the local authorities would have become mere agents or organs of the central government. They object also to the Minister, a politician, having overriding powers in such an intimate and vital matter, since it lays the whole local government structure open to political influence, and may affect the freedom of local councils to be of a different political complexion from the Government. Others will argue that this is a counsel of perfection; that corruption, nepotism and 'sons of the soil' are a brake on progress and efficiency and must be strictly controlled until their influence in West African public life diminishes; and that this control may be regarded as a temporary expedient until West African politics and administration develop greater maturity and impartiality. This is not the place to give a final judgement; our purpose is simply to record a departure from the original intention, and the reasons for it. At the moment it would seem that Western Nigeria is pursuing the middle road, in that the Government controls senior appointments but leaves the councils free to control junior ones; on the other hand, at the time of writing local government in this region is suffering many vicissitudes, and by the time this book is printed there may be radical new developments there.

Secondly, a good working relationship between councillors and staff has rarely been established. Instead of being based on mutual respect and equal partnership it has tended to be a master-servant relationship, based on attempted domination by councillors. This is understandable, but it is necessary to consider the reasons for it.

The true relationship between councillors and officials is not elaborated in the law of local government either in Britain or West Africa, and it would in fact be impossible to define it legally. It is one of those things which is essentially governed by convention rather than by statute, and conventions grow out of local circumstances. It would be absurd to expect the same conventions to grow out of the very different circumstances of West Africa and Britain.

The principal officers of a British local authority are men of high professional standing; as a broad generalization they are probably better educated, better qualified and better paid than many of the councillors whose servants they technically are. Councillors for their part are men and women busy with their own affairs, to whom local government is voluntary public service, and who think too highly of the ability of their officials to want to interfere with them or try to dominate them. Out of these circumstances grows the delicately balanced relationship of working partners, each recognizing the other's authority in their respective spheres.

The principal officers of most West African local authorities are few in number, their professional qualifications are very modest, and they are not highly paid in comparison with civil servants. A high proportion of West African local councillors, on the other hand, are not people of high attainments, many of them are in local government for material gain, and they have little respect for their officials.

Out of these circumstances it is natural that there should grow a different relationship.

This is certainly a case where convention is more important than law, for if a legal definition of the relationship is insisted on it can only be that the council is the master and the officials are its servants, since the council is the statutory authority and the officials (with the reservations we have mentioned) are its employees and agents. But the kind of local government which West Africa has inherited from British tradition will not work on these lines. It results in inefficiency and corruption on the one hand and the continual frustration of officials on the other. This was perhaps the worst miscalculation in importing an alien political institution from Britain. It was easy to import the outward forms, as expressed in legislation, but impossible to import the spirit and the conventions which have taken a long time to grow, and which are the only reason why legislation of this type has proved workable. A narrowly legalistic interpretation can only tend towards domination by councillors who are not fit to dominate, and in circumstances where domination is in any case out of place.

Finally, we come to party politics, a subject which is discussed more fully in the next chapter. Here it is sufficient to say that local government in West Africa is so closely meshed with politics that it is virtually impossible for an official to enjoy the neutrality of his British counterpart. The personal political allegiance of officials is a matter of great interest to the councillors of the majority party; many competent officials have fallen by the wayside because their political allegiance was the wrong one, and many others have had to 'toe a party line' in order to survive and do their work. This is a development which was not anticipated when the first Local Government Ordinances were passed in the early 1950's, but it quickly became apparent and is now taken for granted. It is another fundamental departure from British practice.

So much for the background against which the staffs of

local authorities do their work. The actual nature of this work could only be described satisfactorily in a handbook, or a working manual, and such a description would be out of place in a general survey of this kind; in any case the standing orders and regulations which govern the day-to-day work of officials vary from country to country, and from small rural authorities to large urban ones. Accordingly we will only attempt a few general remarks.

If we are considering the majority of local authorities in West Africa there is not in fact a great deal to be said, since they are small and have very few principal officers, the general nature of whose duties can be understood with a little common sense. The only offices which are common to all local authorities, including the smallest, are those of secretary and treasurer, and even these are sometimes combined in one.

In Britain the chief executive officer is usually described by the old-fashioned title of clerk to the council, but in West Africa the simple word secretary is preferred. The secretary is the general purpose man, who is responsible firstly for the meetings of the council and its committees; secondly for the internal organization of the council offices; and thirdly for the council's dealings with the public and the Government. In the first of these capacities he must summon meetings, prepare the agenda and reports, keep the minutes and other records, and implement the council's decisions; in the second he is responsible for office organization, delegation and co-ordination of work, staff matters and discipline; in his final capacity he negotiates with the Ministry of Local Government, writes the council's letters, conducts interviews on their behalf, deals with contracts and listens to members of the general public. In a small council he will do all this himself, but in larger councils he will have to practise the real art of the administrator, which is delegation; that is to say, another member of his staff may be placed in charge of the work of certain committees, another may be made wholly responsible for minutes and records, another for interviewing members of the public and so on. This kind of delegation grows as the size of the council grows, and in large municipal councils like Freetown, Accra and Lagos the internal organization will become quite elaborate. The basic qualification for the clerk to a council in Britain is that of a solicitor, since he must be familiar with a considerable body of law and must be competent to advise his council upon it. Few secretaries in West Africa outside the big cities have a legal qualification, since neither the responsibilities nor the salaries in local government are yet sufficient to attract such men, but they must nevertheless have a working knowledge not only of the law of local government but of a wide range of Acts or Ordinances which impinge on the work of a local authority. The duties of a secretary are varied, responsible and interesting, and if the authorities were larger in size and financial resources, and if secretaries were able to work free from the interference of councillors or the entanglement of politics, it would be a profession that should attract men of high educational and professional qualifications. But for reasons which we have discussed it is still struggling for prestige, and only in the big cities does it have the status which it deserves, and which it enjoys in more developed countries.

These general remarks apply also to the treasurer, whose responsibilities are narrower but equally onerous; indeed, he usually controls a larger number of subordinate staff because of the continual routine work of revenue collecting, receipting, making and checking of payments, safeguarding of cash and bringing receipts and payments to account. There has been a great deal of financial fraud in local government treasuries, but seen in perspective, and remembering their small salaries and lack of training, treasurers and their staffs deserve a good deal of credit for what they have managed to achieve. Their work, for the most part, is made easier by the fact that government treasuries still insist that they shall follow detailed financial instructions and memoranda, so that the form of their estimates, income and expenditure accounts and balance sheets are closely prescribed, partly in order to assist those who are unskilled in accounting methods and partly to prevent or minimize the possibility of fraud. The treasurer must be thoroughly familiar with these regulations, must be able to advise his council on financial matters, and may have to be prepared to oppose it if he considers its financial decisions unwise or improper; unfortunately this is a situation which arises only too often.

The secretary and treasurer, with the assistants and subordinate staff, comprise the administration; but while no local authority could work without efficient administration, it would be equally true to say that local government would be pointless if it consisted of efficient administration alone. An administration which produced nothing in terms of the welfare of the public would be useless, however internally efficient. Here we come to the current weakness of West African local government, which is its lack of other professional and technical officers. We referred on p. 19 to the immense variety of functions which councils may by law perform, and to the contrast with the narrow range of functions which they do in fact perform because of their lack of qualified staff.

The two basic skills needed in local government are in engineering and public health; but apart from the largest urban authorities, who may employ their own engineer and medical officer, it usually falls to the central government to supply professional knowledge and advice. That is to say a provincial engineer or medical officer will give his services to the local authorities within his area, in addition to carrying out his central responsibilities. In Ghana, a notable attempt has been made to make good the technical deficiencies of local authorities by setting up in three of the eight regions 'Technical Advice Centres', staffed by qualified engineers and architects. Within the local authority itself the highest qualified officer would probably be a works supervisor, assisted by a few artisans such as carpenters, plumbers and motor mechanics, but otherwise only be labourers; or in the field of public health a sanitary or health inspector, a midwife and a dispensary assistant.

The problem is a national rather than a local one. West Africa has far fewer qualified men than it needs. How is the best use to be made of a commodity in short supply—technical skill? Through the agency of central departments or local authorities? This takes us to a question which will be discussed in a later chapter. For the moment we simply record the fact that the average local authority staff consists of a secretary and a treasurer, whose functions we have mentioned; a works supervisor assisted by artisans and labourers, whose work is construction and maintenance—principally of minor roads and bridges, schools, dispensaries and similar buildings; one or more health inspectors, responsible for the prevention of disease by the inspection of refuse and nightsoil disposal, drains and breeding grounds for mosquitoes, and immunization; and, frequently, midwives and dispensary attendants working in the council's own centres.

Local education officers and teachers may also be in a council's employ, but this depends on the division of labour in education between the central and local authorities, usually in the field of primary education. In a sense *all* the work of local authorities turns on this division of labour. The point for the moment is that local authorities are expected to be able to provide, largely out of their own resources but with varying degrees of financial grant aid, the staff necessary for their own administration and for minor public works and public health services.

One final matter which may be touched on in conclusion is the right of local government officials to combine in their own interest through trade union action. The profession of local government in Britain owes much of its status, and officials owe their regular salary scales and conditions of service, to the work of NALGO over sixty years; though it is fair to add that NALGO has always been as insistent on high professional ethical standards as on bargaining for the welfare of its members. We have already seen that the entry of governments into this field, through unified local government services, has to some extent made such activity unnecessary. Nevertheless, attempts have been made in West Africa to form staff associations of various kinds, though like most trade unions they have suffered from poor organization, an unwillingness on the part of members to pay subscriptions, and consequently a weak bargaining position. More successful efforts have been made of recent years to form 'Associations of Local Authorities', which are not quite the same thing as trade unions. They really stand for the interests of local authorities as such, rather than for the welfare of employees. Their function in Britain, where they exist under such names as the Association of Municipal Corporations and the County Councils Association, is to protect the rights and further the interests of local authorities, or of particular kinds of local authorities. It is very largely a parliamentary one—that is to say they keep a careful watch on all legislation which will directly or indirectly affect local authorities, and make representations on appropriate matters to Ministers or departmental officials; further, they have established a position of trust and confidence whereby the Government frequently consults them on local government affairs when legislation is being contemplated or drafted. This is extremely important work, but it is not trade union work, and members of these associations include councillors and officials alike. An association of local authorities, originating in Western Nigeria but spreading to other parts of English-speaking West Africa, is in a sense attempting to combine both functions.

Over the last ten years local government in West Africa has grown visibly in importance, judged solely by the amount of public money which is channelled through it; it has not grown correspondingly in stature and prestige, or established itself as a profession comparable in importance with the Civil Service. A responsible professional association or trade union could be one of the main instruments in remedying this situation.

CHAPTER 5

Party Politics

MOST books on British local government include towards the end a short chapter on the place of party politics in local government. This reflects their relative importance in the local government scene, because although they are of great significance in the affairs of the larger councils they do not occupy that central position which is accorded to them in West Africa; especially is this true of the smaller urban and district councils with which the West African ones can best be compared. So overwhelming is the importance of party politics in West African local government, however, that a chapter on the subject deserves a more prominent place, even though it need not be very long; for here we have another radical departure from what used to be called the British model.

It is a fact often noticed by West African observers that elections in the county boroughs, counties and many municipal councils in Britain are fought on a basis of party politics. What sometimes escapes the observers is the true significance of this fact. Party politics entered local government in Britain when local authorities began to handle affairs of national importance on which Conservatives, Socialists and Liberals normally differ. They do not normally differ, on grounds of political ideology, on such matters as disposing of refuse, keeping the streets clean, repairing the roads, or providing markets, maternity and child welfare centres, pure water supplies, public transport or other amenities; though with the growth of a complex urban civilization differences can begin to appear even in some of these. But broadly speaking what was required was honest and efficient administration, and over a very wide area of local authority work right-wing Conservatives and left-wing Socialists would be hard put to it to discover reasons, based on political belief, for disagreeing with each other. Consequently, in the earlier days of local government little was heard of party politics and the majority of councillors were simply people who wanted their neighbourhood to be well provided for.

But the growth of party politics in British local government was inevitable, and proper, because local authorities carry the main burden of administration in most of the major social services, and their responsibilities now go far beyond providing non-controversial amenities; they must prepare long-term schemes for education, slum clearance, town planning and housing, the use and development of land, and the provision of services like water, electricity and hospitals which have a national rather than a local implication; the last two have in fact been 'nationalized', that is responsibility for them has been transferred from local to central government because they could only be effectively provided for over a wider area than that covered by a local council. In matters of this magnitude it is sensible that local politics should reflect national politics. There are, for example, very real differences in political belief about what sort of education system there should be, whether land and property should be compulsorily acquired in the public interest, or what proportion of houses should be built by public and private enterprise; and these are all matters in which the larger local councils have a considerable measure of independent responsibility.

The point is that whether party politics in local government is right or wrong depends on what the councils do. In West Africa this has not been a relevant consideration; in the first place, few councils perform duties which have more than a local significance; in the second, political parties do not in fact differ on how things should be done, but simply on who should do them.

A study of the minute book of almost any council will show that the greater part of the business of the council and its committees is concerned with such matters as the appointment and personal affairs of the staff, councillors' allowances, the award of contracts, the repair of roads, the allocation of market stalls and comparable matters. None of them could be called political in the sense that there are different *ideological* points of view as to how they should be done and who should do them. It is difficult to suppose, for example, that there is an Action Group and an NCNC method of sweeping the market, cutting the grass and filling in holes in the road; yet some small councils which do little more than this do it in an atmosphere of bitter political warfare. This leads to the second point, that political parties in Nigeria and Sierra Leone[1] are not divided from each other by social and economic policies and beliefs, but by personalities and ethnic rivalries. The fight to win local council elections does not turn on establishing rival plans for social progress, but on entrenching a party in power in a particular locality and winning appointments and perquisites for party supporters. Local councils tend to resemble what in Britain would be called the 'constituency organizations' of a party. The point is worth dwelling on for a moment. In any British town there will be a town council, which may have either a Conservative or a Socialist majority; but if it is a large town, and the centre of a parliamentary constituency, the Conservative and Labour paries may well have local offices and professional party organizers, whose function is to keep the local party organization in good repair, raise funds, recruit members, disseminate propaganda and prepare to win the next general election. There is, however, no connection between, say the Conservative town council and the local headquarters of the Conservative party. In the first the Conservative councillors hammer out, under the criticism of their Socialist opponents, how to provide the *town* with

[1] Ghana, being committed to a one-party system of government, hardly comes into the discussion at this point.

social services; in the other they plan to defeat the Socialists at the next general election in the *parliamentary constituency*. This might or might not correspond with the area of the local authority; in a large town there might be two or more parliamentary constituencies, whereas a small town might be incorporated in a much larger rural area.

In West Africa, on the other hand, the council tends to *become* the constituency party organization.

The difference may be illustrated by another important convention, which is widely, though not universally, observed in Britain. In a 'borough', that is a town which has a mayor, it is customary either for the mayor to come from the majority party and the deputy mayor from the minority one, or for the two parties to hold the office in turn; this symbolizes the fact that the mayor is the chief representative citizen and is to that extent above politics. Similarly, it is customary either to share the chairmanships of committees between the parties, or to arrange that the chairman comes from one party and the vice-chairman from another; it is also customary to spread the membership of the committees proportionately between the parties. Incidentally, it is the general experience that in committees dealing with the down-to-earth work of local government party differences tend to evaporate, while in small councils dealing with purely local matters they hardly exist at all; in such councils there is still room for the politically independent member.

The contrast in West African councils is sharp. Not only does the winning party take all the chairmanships, but unless restrained they will appoint only party members to committees; we have already seen (p. 36) that the Western Nigerian Government was compelled to include a section in its local government law enabling the Minister to use powers of direction if it appeared to him 'that the minority parties are not adequately represented on a committee of the council'; otherwise they might well have been excluded altogether. The power of the majority party pervades every aspect of a council's life and work, even to the extent of compelling the council's employees to join the party under threat of dismissal.

In general, throughout this book, we are not concerned to criticize departures from British practice; indeed, we have several times stressed the point that foreign institutions cannot be imported with any hope of success unless they are applied flexibly and are readily adapted to suit local circumstances and tradition, and most of the adaptations that have been made so far are more suitable than the original. We are tempted to make an exception here, because the influence of party politics on local government is so manifestly bad. Councils are diverted from their proper purposes; members or supporters of other parties are victimized; and no moderation is shown. Until recently one would have said that there was no point in complaining about this, or even discussing it, because party politics were in local government to stay and nothing could be done about it. There are, however, signs of a reaction. Leading Nigerians in particular are realizing that the country will gain nothing at home, and will earn discredit abroad, if the present situation continues, and the Premier of the Eastern Region has recently (February 1963) made an important speech drawing attention to this and affirming his Government's resolve to keep politics out of local government so far as it is in their power to do so.

We do not suggest that the problem is easy or straightforward, because if local government develops to the extent of administering services of national importance, and of a controversial kind, party politics will come to have a legitimate place. Even now, people in West Africa ask how local authorities can act as agents of the central government if they have a different political loyalty. This question makes two assumptions; first, that political beliefs are involved in the matters on which governments and local authorities deal with one another, which is, as we have seen, largely untrue; second, that the local authorities are in fact agents of the central government, which is only partly true. Nevertheless, it is a fact that in Britain as elsewhere a special difficulty may arise when a council of one political complexion has to carry out the policies of a government of another; it need not necessarily arise, because a great deal of the work involved between them is non-controversial; but it can very well arise, and frequently does so. A high proportion of town councils in Britain today have Socialist majorities, whereas the Government is a Conservative one, and occasionally they have had sharp differences.

When this happens the only solution is moderation and restraint. The Government must, of course, have the final word, since there can only be one sovereign authority in the state, since local councils draw their own authority from Parliament, and since they depend to a large extent on the Government for money. But a government, of whatever party, will be careful not to prevent councils from following their own convictions, and not to compel them to act against these convictions, except in matters which they consider to be really vital; local councils for their part will acknowledge the authority of the government of the day, and will not seek to press differences to the point of deadlock or collapse. In West Africa it is all too common for those who have to accept something they do not like to 'walk out' and refuse to take any further part in the proceedings; this does nothing to further either the welfare of their constituents or the cause of democracy.

It is often thought that compromise of this kind is a typically British escape from a difficult situation, that the British have elevated it to a virtue among their own people, and that they have no business to force it down the throats of Africans. It is significant, therefore, that one of the best statements of the principle involved has been made not from British sources but by the Premier of the Northern Region of Nigeria, in 1958. In a message headed 'Declaration by the government of the Northern Region on its relations with native authorities', the Sardauna of Sokoto says:

'During the recent tours of the Premier, at some places

he was asked to clarify the position of native authorities and the Regional government in a self-governing Northern Region, and therefore the Premier takes this chance to make the stand of the government known not only to those who asked but to everybody in the Region.

'In every country where there are democratic institutions the relationship between the Government in power and local government bodies is bound to present certain problems. Nigeria is no exception to this rule. The Regional government therefore believes that a clear statement of its policy on this subject will be of value in allaying any doubts which may exist among native authorities and political parties of the Opposition.

'The government of the Northern Region recognizes that, just as the constitution provides different spheres of activity for the Federal government on the one hand and the Regional government on the other, so the law defines separate fields for the Regional government on the one hand and the native authorities on the other. Within the field of local government, the Regional government is ready to grant native authorities complete freedom of action provided always that certain essential conditions are observed. These conditions are that native authorities should retain the confidence of the great mass of their people, that they should discharge adequately the duties and responsibilities assigned to them, that they should conduct their financial affairs in a prudent and responsible fashion, and that they should maintain the standards of honesty and impartiality required in a country approaching independence.

'The Regional government, which is ultimately responsible for law, order and sound administration must, however, reserve to itself the right to intervene in local government matters if these conditions are not met. This right is recognized by the law which has provided certain overriding powers. These are financial, executive and legal, and they vary in range from the ability to withhold a small grant to the power of the Governor-in-Council to annul the appointment of any native authority.

'Wide as these powers are, however, they cannot be arbitrarily exercised. They are subject to two great sanctions of democratic representative government, namely the rule of law and freedom of discussion. Native authorities are constituted under and safeguarded by legal processes and any government which sought to suppress them or encroach upon their statutory rights would have to proceed according to law. Such a move, whether justified or not, would be reported in the Press and could be made the subject of a debate in the regional legislature. Consequently any government which took action against a native authority from improper motives would risk exposure at the bar of public opinion.

'These are the safeguards which democracy provides to preserve the weak against the strong and they are just as important in constitutional as in human relationships. The Regional government affirms its faith in these safeguards and pledges itself to observe them in the spirit as well as the letter. In particular it is resolved to treat all native authorities, irrespective of their political sympathies, with strict impartiality and scrupulously to refrain from any action which could be attributed to political bias. Native authorities may therefore rest assured that, provided that they for their part discharge their statutory and moral obligations, they will not be subject to unjustifiable interference or undue influence by the Regional government.'

This sums up the situation admirably.

Finally, it must not be thought that party politics have entered British local government, at any level, without protest or regret. Two main arguments have been advanced against them; first, that the need to be sponsored as a candidate by a political party has robbed local government of the services of many men and women who would have been an asset to it, but who belong to no political party, or at any rate are not politically active; and second, that party organization within the council, with its 'caucus' and its voting on strict party lines, robs the council debates of any reality and means that all the decisions are taken in advance. The first of these arguments is a substantial one in a country where many citizens of great ability and public spirit have not the obsessive interest in politics that one finds in West Africa; the second applies equally to the House of Commons; the argument and discussion out of which policy is shaped take place within the party and not within the whole elected body, and there is both loss and gain in this.

But the argument that the *major* local authorities are now dealing with matters which may properly be called political is conclusive; added to which party politics have added a good deal of interest and zest to the work of local councils, and, judging from the proportion of electors who take the trouble to vote in local elections (never very high), have also increased the interest of the electorate.

But to repeat, and in conclusion, two conditions need to be observed; first, that party politics are confined to matters which are in essence political, and should not be allowed to dominate every aspect of a local authority's work, much less affect the staff and the routine work; and second, that political power should be used with moderation, and that councillors of the opposition should not be excluded from a fair share of responsibility. If local councils became replicas of Parliament, which they were never intended to be, with Opposition members having no function but to oppose, local government would lose its present character. It is indeed losing its former character in some of the larger cities of Britain, where the dominant party keeps a firm grip on all the controls, and does not observe the inter-party conventions which were mentioned earlier in this chapter.

The logical conclusion of this *could* be local parliamentary government, with councillors in charge of departments and the apparatus of a Cabinet. Some people in Britain forsee this as a possible development, though most would regret it. But at least it would make sense in the context of what these city councils have to do; in the West African context it would make no sense at all, and would simply mean that local government in the intention of the existing local government laws had been abandoned, and something else substituted in its place.

CHAPTER 6

The Work of Local Authorities

WE have already referred several times to the work of the local councils, since it has only been possible to write about their structure, their membership and their staff in terms of what they actually do; but we must now try to describe this work more fully and systematically. It falls into two main categories:

(a) exercising their powers and duties (under the instruments by which they are established) to provide a wide variety of services;

(b) making by-laws to fulfil and enforce their decisions.

POWERS AND DUTIES

It is not easy to describe the functions of local authorities simply and unambiguously, because some of them, including the most important, are closely bound up with the functions of central government departments; moreover, some powers are mandatory, i.e. they are compulsory duties, while others are permissive, i.e. councils may perform them or not as they wish. The local government laws of the three countries we are considering set them out in different ways. The Eastern Nigerian Law of 1960 is convenient for our purpose because it includes a long and exhaustive list of every function that may be performed by a local authority, though if one wishes to know what any *particular* council may do it would be necessary to refer to the Instrument establishing it; this list is additionally convenient for the layman because it is broken up into types or categories of work. The list in the Western Nigerian Law is much shorter, because the law is drafted on a different principle. Instead of giving an exhaustive list of everything that local authorities may in certain circumstances do, it gives a much shorter list of purposes for which they may 'maintain works and services'; this acknowledges the fact that the responsibility for much of the work done by local councils is a central and not a local government responsibility, and that the Government takes the councils 'into partnership'. For example, the Western Law makes no mention of education, although in practice the councils spend a great deal of their energies on schools; this is because the relevant legislation is found elsewhere, in the Education Law, which provides that much of the administration of education shall be conducted through 'local education authorities', which means in practice suitable local councils. Again, although Western Nigeria, like the North but unlike the East, maintains *local authority* police forces, the Local Government Act has nothing to say about them because the powers of local authorities in respect of police are dealt with in a separate Police Law. The Ghanaian Act of 1961 is different again; its lists, in a Schedule to the Act, thirty functions which are mandatory upon all *city and municipal* councils; it then follows this up with a much longer list of seventy-eight functions which *may* be included in the Instrument setting up *any* council; this underlines the point made on p. 21 that certain urban services are inescapable, whereas rural services may be performed or not according to local circumstances, and without disastrous results if they are not performed.

These three methods of defining the functions of local authorities in the law have their advantages and disadvantages, but for the purposes of this book there is no need to labour the point, since the end result is much the same. For the layman, there are obvious advantages in taking as an example the Eastern Nigerian Law, since that gives the most comprehensive view of what is possible; this does not mean that it is better drafted than the other laws, but simply that because of the method it adopts it gives the easiest and most comprehensive bird's-eye view. The Law gives the main categories of a local council's potential work in alphabetical order, as follows:

Agriculture

Powers are provided for improving agriculture and controlling methods of husbandry.

Animals

This heading includes some simple things like controlling the movements of animals, and more difficult ones like improving the quality of stock and preventing disease.

Powers in respect of both agriculture and livestock are common to all West African local government laws, but they are not very widely given in Instruments or used by councils, who show little interest in them. In Eastern Nigeria the county councils, taken together, only spent upon them 0·4 per cent and 0·2 per cent of their total expenditure in a recent year. Both lie much more within the province of the Department of Agriculture, since they require professional knowledge and skill which are not available to the local authorities. There are from time to time proposals to remove them altogether from local government, for the councils can do little more than establish small demonstration plots, or nurseries for seeds, or carry out simple instructions from the Ministry.

Buildings

These, together with 'roads and streets', which are listed separately, are much nearer to the heart of a local authority's work, and in Eastern Nigeria recently consumed 27 per cent of total expenditure. Apart from actual construction, e.g. of schools, dispensaries, maternity centres, shops, rest houses, etc., powers under this head include important ones of planning. Local authorities may lay down conditions about design, layout and building lines, and may undertake new housing schemes; they may also control old buildings, either from the point of view of sanitation or safety. This is important work, most of it grantaided, and makes a significant contribution to the total construction programme in the Region. The Ministry of Public Works is of course responsible for major undertakings, especially those requiring architectural or engineering knowledge, such as elaborate buildings or heavy traffic bridges, and the Ministry also gives technical advice as far as the time of their staff allows. But it is under this heading that the local authorities, through their own supervisors, artisans and labourers, make their most concrete contribution to national development, both in the literal and metaphorical sense of the word; it must be added, regrettably, that it is in the award of contracts for building projects that most corruption has taken place.

Education

This is the function which arouses most interest and consumes the highest proportion of local government expenditure (32 per cent in Eastern Nigeria, compared with 27 per cent on works); there is indeed a danger of councils showing too much interest in education, to the detriment of their other responsibilities, since it is at least arguable that public health measures, including above all supplies of pure water, are as important for nation-building as primary education. However, as facts are, it is the responsibility which interests councils throughout West Africa more than anything else.

Arrangements in Eastern Nigeria and Ghana vary in detail, but they have it in common that local authorities may both 'build, equip, maintain and manage' schools themselves, and also make financial grants to enable others to do so.[1] The law does not restrict local authorities to primary schools, but in practice, for obvious reasons of capital costs and staff salaries, few secondary schools or teacher training colleges are managed by local councils.

[1] The Ghana Local Government Act omits the second in the case of city and municipal councils; that is to say all new schools must be local authority schools, and must be established on the direction of the Minister of Education. Outside the municipalities both provisions exist.

A high proportion (about four-fifths in Eastern Nigeria) of primary schools belong to voluntary agencies or churches, who accordingly depend on the local councils for a proportion of their recurrent costs, which not infrequently brings them into financial difficulties. In Western Nigeria, as we have said, local authorities have no specific educational powers in their own right, but are in practice 'local education authorities' of the Ministry of Education for all purposes, and have local education officers attached to their staff.

In addition, both in Southern Nigeria and Ghana local councils or local educational authorities may grant scholarships or bursaries to attend 'any schools or other educational institutions in the home country or elsewhere', and the Eastern Nigerian definition of educational facilities extends to 'public libraries, museums, or associations for the promotion of arts, crafts, recreation and sport'.

Forestry

This refers to tree nurseries, forest plantations and forest reserves, and the selling of their produce. It is an important function from the point of view of preserving natural resources, but as with *Agriculture* and *Animals* local councils show little interest in it (the amount spent in Eastern Nigeria in the year quoted is virtually nil). There is a widespread opinion that it is an inappropriate function for local councils and should be a direct responsibility of the Forestry Department.

Liquor

This section deals with the 'prohibiting, restricting, regulating or licensing the manufacture, sale, distribution, supply, possession and consumption of palm wine and all kinds of fermented liquor usually made by Nigerians', and requires no comment.

Markets

These sections bring us to an altogether more important

function. In Britain markets are a somewhat minor responsibility of local government, though urban authorities are responsible for them and indeed employ Markets Managers of relatively senior status; but rural markets do not exist in such profusion as in West Africa and markets generally do not occupy such an important place in the life of the community; throughout Africa they are not only of economic but of social importance, and much of the life of the country revolves round them. In Eastern Nigeria they occupied fourth place among the services provided, and accounted for over 3 per cent of total expenditure. The responsibilities of local councils include building and maintaining them, allocating and fixing the rent for stalls (alas, the second most fruitful source of corruption in local government) and fixing the days and hours of their opening.

Public Health

This is even more important, occupying third place in the services provided (after education and works) and accounting for over 9 per cent of expenditure. In Britain it could perhaps be said to have been the foundation of nineteenth-century local government, and today it represents the hard core of the work of the minor authorities (urban and rural district councils). In Nigeria, unlike Britain, it is a service shared between the local authorities, the Ministry of Health, whose medical officers carry a good deal of the work which requires high professional skill, and the Ministry of Works, who provide hospitals, water supplies, drainage schemes and other installations which require expensive equipment and technical skill. Nevertheless, the direct responsibilities of local councils are varied and important; they include, briefly, maternity homes, dispensaries and ambulances; control of vermin; disposal of nightsoil and refuse; local water supplies; slaughter houses and the inspection of animals and meat; cemeteries and burial grounds; and the control and inspection of the manufacture of food and drink. These may seem rather uninteresting duties, and they are certainly far removed from the excitement and glamour of party political warfare, but they are none the less the inescapable and basic responsibilities of local government; the community would suffer seriously if they were neglected, whereas it would not suffer very much if one political party were knocked out by another. The community owes a great debt to the health inspectors and sanitary labourers employed by local councils, and their work deserves higher recognition and status than it gets.

Public Order

All councils, quite irrespective of this part of the law, have a duty to 'generally maintain order and good government', and this point will be discussed later in the chapter; but these sections under *Public Order* give councils specific powers to deal with natural nuisances such as fires, and man-made nuisances such as brothels, gambling, begging, hawking and making various kinds of noise.

Registration of Persons

This principally refers to the compulsory registration of births, marriages and deaths, and is not at the time of writing operated by many local authorities in the Region. Indeed, it hardly exists throughout Nigeria, and in Ghana it is only enforced in certain urban areas. For many years people have said that it would be a desirable step to make it universal, but that the practical difficulties were insuperable; curiously enough it is operated throughout Sierra Leone, in the so-called 'chiefdoms' (which are the lower tier of local authorities) without, apparently, giving rise to any insuperable problems. There is of course a good deal of prejudice against its introduction, based on misconceptions.

Although this is not one of the functions of most local authorities at the moment it could ultimately become one of the most significant of them. One of the great barriers to progress and development in West Africa is lack of information, and particularly of vital statistics, i.e. statistics of population and age structure; without registration it is also impossible to keep contemporary records (e.g. electoral rolls) up to date, and the absence of certificates of birth, marriage or death will cause increasing difficulty to tens of thousands of people as government welfare schemes develop. The elaborate social security schemes in other countries depend upon the kind of information which registration provides, and also upon the individual being able to produce proof of identity, date of birth, marriage or the death of next of kin. The point is therefore worth this small digression.

Roads, Streets, etc.

These, together with *Buildings*, form the hard core of the work of the engineering staff. There are two aspects to it, rural and urban; the first involves making and maintaining 'bush' roads, or in the words of the law 'roads other than Federal trunk roads'; in practice this means unmetalled roads, as few local authorities have the equipment for tarring; the second involves lighting, cleaning and draining as well as construction and maintenance, and also providing car and lorry parks and regulating the traffic; in certain parts of the country the operation of ferries is also important. These sections, incidentally, give local authorities power to licence bicycles and other vehicles, apart from motor vehicles.

Trade and Industry

These sections are principally concerned with *regulation*, that is with prescribing the conditions under which certain trades and industries may be carried on; they relate to offensive and dangerous trades, and to the manufacture and sale of food; also to checking weights and measures, and to controlling hotels and catering establishments.

They do also however, permit local authorities to 'establish and operate secondary industries' themselves. They do not in fact do this, except in one or two places and in a very small way, and the provision is not included in the laws of Western Nigeria and Ghana. Its presence here does, however, raise an important question of principle—whether it is a proper function of local authorities to engage in trade or industry for profit. Some people say that they should confine themselves to providing public services out of the rates, or amenities for which a direct fee may be paid by the user, such as for the use of a lorry park or swimming bath; others say that if they are capable of adding to the wealth and productive capacity of their neighbourhood they should do so, as West Africa is a poor country and every little helps; also, that the more prosperous an area is the more the local authority will be able to raise in local rates for other amenities. There is no 'right' or 'wrong' in this matter; 'municipal trading', as it is called, was once popular in Britain as a principle, but has made no headway and has little significance today. Perhaps the decisive point against it is that all productive enterprise involves risk, and elected representatives handling public money compulsorily obtained out of the rates should not indulge in risk.

There is a final category headed *Various Matters*, but this need not detain us, since the foregoing categories give a fairly good idea of the *scope* of the work which is usually associated with local government. Later on we shall be discussing whether these are necessarily the appropriate functions of local government, whether local authorities should do more or less, and on what grounds; and whether anything is gained by putting these or other services under the control of locally elected citizens. Here we are merely describing what exists.

We have summarized the functions of local authorities in general terms for the sake of simplicity, but in the laws themselves they are set out at length and in precise detail. This fact is important because local authorities may only do what the law specifically says they may do, and if they went beyond this they would be held to have acted *ultra vires*, and expenditure would have been incurred illegally. This legal doctrine is the opposite of the one which applies to the individual, who may do anything he pleases unless and until he breaks a law; the law does not say what he may do but what he may not do; with local authorities it is the other way round.

There is, however, one general duty laid upon all local authorities, which cannot be listed as a specific function or defined with any precision; that is the duty generally to assist in maintaining order and good government. The Nigerian laws go further and make it an obligation on every council and every individual member of a council to do their best to prevent crime or breaches of the peace, and individual councillors may be punished if they fail to take certain steps, such as reporting to the proper authorities, and carrying out the orders of a police officer or justice of the peace as a result of this.

In Western, as in Northern, Nigeria their responsibility for law and order is emphasized by the fact that they have their own police forces. The Local Government Police Law of 1955 allows this, subject to the approval of the Minister in every case, and the local government police perform a lot of useful minor functions and supplement the work of the Federal police, especially in the proceedings of customary courts and in routine work such as serving official documents and regulating traffic. Their existence in Nigeria is a controversial subject and was hotly debated at the constitutional conferences which preceded independence. Their critics say that they are illiterate and badly trained by comparison with the Nigerian police; that they are the tools of the political party which controls the council, and are used by them to oppress their opponents; and that they are corrupt. The other side of the argument is that at Nigeria's present stage of development a lot of minor police work does not need high qualifications or training; that it would indeed be a misuse of the time of the highly trained men, who are all too few in number; and that as long as customary courts remain alongside the magistrates courts it is logical that there should be police forces to correspond. There are, however, no local authority police forces in Eastern Nigeria, and the work done by the so-called 'court messengers' is not comparable to that of the other local police forces. It is not easy to explain why local police forces are considered essential in Western, but not in Eastern Nigeria; the case of Northern Nigeria is different, as there are few Nigerian (Federal) police stationed there.

The Ghana Local Government Act also provides for local police forces, and defines their function as maintaining and safeguarding public order and the safety of persons and property (for which they have powers of arrest); executing processes arising out of local courts; and assisting the Ghana police.

The control of a police force is therefore a fairly normal function of local government in West Africa.

In the days of colonial administration the 'native authority' was almost synonymous with the 'native court', but in recent years the tendency has been to separate the administration of justice from the administration of services, and members of the customary courts, as they are now called in Nigeria (local courts in Ghana) are appointed by the Minister of Justice or his representative, and their work has nothing to do with that of the local council. Local authorities are, however, responsible for maintaining the local court, which is similar to the arrangement in Britain; and, unlike Britain, fines, fees and other court proceeds form part of the revenue of the councils and appear in the estimates of income and expenditure. A few local authorities still maintain a prison also, an inheritance from the days of native administration, but the tendency is for these to be taken over by the national police.

BY-LAWS

Local councils, then, are constantly deciding that a great variety of things shall be done, and many of their decisions involve the ordinary person in obeying their orders. This is only possible if the councils have local legislative powers and are able to enforce the local laws which they make.

Accordingly, local government legislation confers upon

them the power to make 'by-laws', which must be obeyed under penalties not exceeding a fine of £25–£50 or imprisonment for 3–6 months.[1]

It is not easy for amateur legislators like councillors to make proper by-laws, and the process is carefully safeguarded. No by-law of a local council can become effective until it has been approved by the Minister, and this provision is necessary for a number of reasons. First, the Government's legal advisers must make sure that the proposed by-law is *intra vires*, i.e. within the council's competence to make; secondly it must be in correct legal form; and finally it must not conflict with any other law or by-law, made by any legally constituted authority, within the area of the council's jurisdiction. Because of these difficulties it is the practice of governments to publish 'model' or 'adoptive' by-laws on subjects which are of common interest to large numbers of councils; it is then only necessary for the council to 'adopt' this particular by-law, and all the trouble over drafting and investigation is saved.[2]

The nature of most by-laws follows naturally from the functions of local authorities. If examples are required, in order to give a mental picture of the scope of local legislation, the Western Nigerian Local Government Law is most helpful, as it gives a list of no fewer than thirty-nine matters, in five broad categories, on which by-laws may be made. We take a few typical examples from each:

Natural Resources

Controlling disease in trees, crops or plants; the movement of livestock; fencing; rules about cultivation.

Markets

Goods which may or may not be sold; rents and fees; inspection of produce offered for sale; weights and measures; maximum prices.

[1] The laws vary in detail on this point.

[2] In the same way it is the practice to issue 'model standing orders' and 'model contracts'.

Roads and Transport

Obstruction of drains or watercourses; planting and destroying of trees; demolition of dangerous buildings; licensing of bicycles and carrying of lights; naming and numbering of streets; advertisements.

Public Order

Control of firearms, weapons, noise, gambling, begging, hawking, etc.

Miscellaneous

Licensing of entertainments, registration of births, deaths and marriages, intoxicating liquor.

It will be seen at a glance that the matters on which councils may make by-laws (or rather on which Instruments may convey the power to make by-laws) in Western Nigeria follows very closely the list of *functions* in Eastern Nigeria. As we remarked earlier, the two laws simply approach the matter in slightly different ways.

CONTRACTS

Another activity which arises constantly from the ordinary work of a council is the award of contracts, either for buildings or for the purchase of goods. In order to prevent fraud by irresponsible councils, of which there has unfortunately been a great deal, these awards are controlled by governments, and large contracts have to be approved by the Minister, who makes certain that they have been put out honestly to tender, that the best tender is recommended for acceptance, and that councillors voting to award contracts have no personal or financial interest in them. In Western Nigeria and Ghana the maximum contract which a council may award on its own authority is £2,000 (£5,000 in Ghanaian municipalities); in Eastern Nigeria it is much lower.

This chapter has been little more than a précis, with comments, of the more important matters which are common to the three Laws or Acts. Its purpose has been to give the reader a general idea of what the activity called local government is about. All the points which have been touched on have been simplified, and several matters have been omitted. Those who want to understand a little more of the complexity of local government administration would need to study the local government law of the country in which they live, using this chapter as an introduction.

CHAPTER 7

The Size and Population of Local Authorities

THIS chapter is concerned with the competence of local authorities to perform their functions, and it introduces problems which have never yet been satisfactorily solved in any country, and which indeed may never be finally solved since their nature is constantly changing. We come up against the fact that local government is not a rigid system, but must constantly be changing with the rise of standards and the advance of technology. To summarize these problems in advance:

The size, and more particularly the population, of a local authority determines its revenue; this in turn will determine what it is capable and what it is not capable of doing; moreover, some of the functions of local authorities can be efficiently and economically administered over a small area, whereas others require a large one; as a further complication, some of those which need only a small area may come to need a larger one, as technical efficiency grows through new methods and discoveries; consequently, the administering authority may have to combine with others, in order to become bigger, or alternatively lose the administration of such functions altogether and allow them to be administered by a larger authority, such as a provincial, regional or national government. A related problem is that some functions which *can* be performed satisfactorily over a small area (e.g. a town) nevertheless need highly qualified staff, which a small authority cannot afford.

In any country in the world this problem arises—that different functions need different areas for their economical and efficient administration. Unless, therefore, there is to be a separate authority for every function there is bound to be a compromise between what is most efficient and economical on the one hand, and what is likely to be acceptable to the local people on the other. Even if—to carry the argument to an absurd point—a separate authority were to be established for every function, the problems of overlapping that this would create would outweigh the advantage gained from the best administration of each individual function. Moreover, the representative idea, which has always been thought to be important in English-speaking West Africa, would diminish, because it would be impossible to have a multiplicity of elected authorities for several different purposes.

Hitherto, a compromise has been made through the device of arranging local government in 'tiers', so that functions are divided between larger and smaller authorities. But in Southern Nigeria and Ghana even the upper tiers lack the necessary resources to meet their obligations, and in any case the tier system, though it has worked satisfactorily in Britain, has been the cause of endless friction and suspicion in West Africa, and has now largely been done away with. To have more than one local authority working on the same ground, one of which may 'precept', that is issue financial demands, upon another, has proved unacceptable to councils and public alike.

Let us try to reduce these generalizations to more practical terms by looking at the recent experience of Britain; we shall then be able to see how, in a simpler setting, that experience is being reproduced in contemporary West Africa.

To begin with, the structure of local government in Britain provides West Africa with an awful warning. It has changed very little since it first took shape in the late 1880's and early 1890's; but the sort of world it was designed to serve has changed beyond recognition; horses have given way to motor cars, manual labour to machines, and every kind of communication and administrative technique has accelerated a hundredfold. During this time local authorities have had to undertake a steadily increasing amount of work. In other words British local government is trying to do a mid-twentieth-century job with a late nineteenth-century tool; in particular it is operating in the 1960's with local council areas which were suitable for the conditions of the 1890's.

The result of this has been that a number of important functions which the local authorities used to perform have now been taken away from them and given to larger bodies; and others which used to be performed by the smaller and more numerous local authorities are now performed only by the largest ones.

Examples of the first process are that electricity, gas and hospitals, which used to be important local government services, have now been 'nationalized'; to some extent this was inevitable, since Britain is a small country, and as technical improvements were made in, for example, generating and distributing electricity, it was sensible that the service should be administered nationally and not locally; on the other hand local authorities would not have lost all such powers if they themselves had been growing and adapting; at any rate they might have continued to have some share in their administration, whereas now the Government, having nationalized these services, has decentralized their administration to 'Regional Boards', covering much larger areas than the local government ones; these bodies are not elected by the people but nominated by the Minister in charge of the particular function; thus representative democracy has taken a step backwards.

It is, of course, arguable that there is no advantage in having our electricity supplies or our hospitals controlled by the directly elected representatives of the people, except in as far as they are both ultimately controlled by Parliament, which is the supreme elected body. Why not let them be controlled by competent officials? As long as electricity can be switched on, at a reasonable price, does it matter who controls the organization which makes this possible? As long as a sick person can be moved to hospital, does it matter how the hospital gets there? To most people, frankly, it matters very little, and it is possible that Britain has clung too long to a tradition of local control over matters which are not in essence local.

A good example of the second process—the transfer of functions from smaller to larger local authorities—is the fire brigades, though there are many others. Early in the century a fire engine was a simple affair drawn by a horse, and there would be one in every small town or village, since they could not travel very far or very fast. Nowadays fleets of fire engines, wonderfully equipped, can travel fifty miles in a very short time, and telecommunications can summon them from far and wide. But they are very expensive, and only the larger authorities can afford them, so fire fighting ceases to be a function of the smaller councils; indeed, as a result of experience in the 1939-45 war a good deal of its control is now national.

What this amounts to is that progress brings with it a need for larger units of administration and a tendency towards centralization, and representative local government can only keep pace with this—if it is thought desirable for it to do so—if its own boundaries are being adjusted and enlarged.

What has happened in Britain, in a nutshell, is that a river has overflowed its banks; services which needed to flow through a broad channel were confined to a narrow ditch, so that they burst their banks and found their own level. The result is rather curious, because it has caused the history of a hundred years ago to repeat itself. In the nineteenth century, before the present local authorities were designed, the different services *were* in fact administered by a number of single-purpose bodies, generally known as Boards; there were elected Boards for administering the poor law, public health, schools, highways and other matters; this was thought to be wasteful and inefficient, and the gathering together of these services under multi-purpose authorities was thought to be a great improvement But now that a number of services have broken out of the confines of local government, there is once again a bewildering array of different kinds of authorities doing different things—regional boards, joint boards of several local authorities, *ad hoc* boards which recognize no previous statutory boundaries, but which are created to conform to the natural area of the work they do, such as drainage, water supply and river control.

The existence of the problem is illustrated by the fact that for the last twenty years persistent efforts have been made to reform local government boundaries, so that functions and areas, which are really inseparable, should correspond to each other better than they do now. Local Government Boundary Commissions have been at work since the end of the 1939–45 war, but one was disbanded without having achieved any concrete results, and the others are only now beginning to produce any proposals, which are nearly always strongly resisted by the councils concerned. The fact is that when a system of local government has been allowed to set in a hard mould, and when an increasing amount of work has been placed upon it, it becomes a very hard administrative problem, and a very sensitive political problem, to alter it. It is essential that the local government laws in developing countries should be flexible, so that the areas and boundaries of local government can be more easily adjusted to meet changing circumstances.

Before turning to the specific problems of West Africa, it must be added that the arguments we have just outlined do not mean that local government is in decline, or that all its work is passing to the larger authorities, regional or national; the hard core of local government, comprising services which concern only a town or a small rural area, will always remain; and many matters of high national importance such as education and public health are still administered by the eighty-year-old county boroughs and county councils with imagination and success. On the other hand it needs to be realized that what is suitable today may not be suitable ten years hence, and that both the areas and functions of local government need to be kept under constant review. Some of the county boroughs and counties are either too small to be effective or too large for representative local democracy.

When we turn to look at the size and population of local

authorities in Southern Nigeria and Ghana we find that, apart from the big municipalities, they are too small to be able to do many of the things which the local government laws theoretically permit them to do. This does not mean that they are useless; it simply means that the central departments of government are doing a great deal more, and the local authorities a great deal less, than was originally intended.

The revenue of the average country or district council is, let us say, in the neighbourhood of £40,000, including government grants-in-aid. The cost of administration may absorb some 15–20 per cent of this, and it has to be remembered that the salaries of the staff are very modest. The mere maintenance of what already exists—local roads, schools, health centres—may absorb the bulk of the rest, even though central government departments are assisting with technical advice and providing major works; what remains can only meet the cost of minor services; and always there is the problem of getting in the tax. In other words these councils can fulfil the function of small urban or rural district councils in Britain, together with their existing responsibilities for schools, but they cannot measure up to most of the possible functions of local authorities as detailed in the laws, because they are too small to produce the necessary revenue. It must be remembered always that they employ no highly qualified staff outside the administration.

The Government of Western Nigeria recently did some research into this problem, and came to the conclusion that the optimum area over which to administer education was one which contained between 550 and 600 primary schools, taking account of the staff that was needed for teaching, inspection and maintenance; and that an area which contained less than 100 primary schools would be both uneconomic and inefficient. They applied similar tests to the public health service, and concluded that the optimum was one which employed not less than fifteen health inspectors; one factor which they took into account here was the need to have a big enough staff employed by one agency to allow for internal promotion; the lack of opportunity for promotion in the service of small local authorities is one of their most disheartening features, and one which virtually prevents them from employing staff of any real calibre. Tests of this kind can be applied to all the major services with which local authorities are associated. This is not the place to examine them in any further detail, but two observations can be made about them; first, that only the few biggest authorities came anywhere near the minimum standard for efficiency; second, that the method of approach is in itself of great significance—(a) what is the optimum area for administering a certain service? (b) how near can we get to this optimum, bearing in mind the other factors which have to be taken into account, such as traditional areas, local loyalties, communications and, as always, politics. For local government areas can never achieve the ideal—always there must be a search for a compromise between what will satisfy the people and what will provide efficient and progressive administration.

The difficulty in developing countries, which stands out more sharply than the same difficulty in Britain, is that the mass of people are not sufficiently informed to be able to think of local government at all in terms of areas suitable for efficient administration; while politicians, who *do* understand the problem, are too much swayed by the people on whom they depend for votes, and support small, uneconomical and out-of-date local council areas even when they know they are against the best interests of development. The ordinary man tends to see local government in terms of local feuds, traditional rivalries, and distrust of neighbouring towns or communities with whom he is unwilling to share his own resources, and whom he suspects of getting more than their fair share of benefits; not only does he not want his council to combine with others—he would like it to become still smaller; and the politicians often back him up. Probably the best solution, and one to which Western Nigeria has been slowly working, would be to leave the 'natural' areas, in which peoples' local loyalties reside, untouched; to give them as much to do as possible; but not to give them powers and duties in connection with the major services on which the progress of Nigeria as a nation depends —agriculture and natural resources, public education, public health or major public works. All governments want to avoid the enforcement of unpopular measures, not only for political reasons but because development will flow more smoothly if people are governed by consent; but in countries where there are such great extremes in the level of understanding they may have to be prepared to take their courage in both hands.

One compromise that has long been practised is the institution of 'Joint Committees' or 'Joint Boards'. Joint Committees, which are provided for in all the laws we are considering, are a simple device. It is provided that 'councils may concur, with one or more other councils, in appointing from their respective members a joint committee of the councils for a purpose in which they are jointly interested', and such committees may be given delegated powers, other than legislative or financial powers. This enables councils, by voluntary agreement, to deal with matters which cut across their boundaries or which they can better manage in co-operation; thus a joint committee might be responsible for a water supply which for reasons of local geography could provide water on both sides of a local government boundary line; or (except in Eastern Nigeria) there could be a joint committee for managing a combined local police force.

Joint Boards, which are provided for in the Western Nigerian Law, are altogether more important bodies, and come very near to being a new kind of local authority in their own right. They may be established by voluntary agreement between councils, but normally they are created by Government action—'The Minister may *require* any two or more councils to establish a joint board for any purpose . . .' They have their own Instruments defining their powers and duties, which must be approved by the Minister and gazetted; the 'contributing councils' appoint their own members, but once appointed they are not subject to their councils' direction, but hold office on the board in their own right. Several of the 'local education authorities' in this Region are joint boards of councils, and not the councils themselves.

Here we see the same development that we noted in Britain—the creation of *ad hoc* boards, in the manner of the nineteenth century, for the purpose of performing a certain function which the local authorities individually are not capable of performing properly.

Once this principle is accepted—once, that is to say, it is admitted that the statutory local authorities are inadequate for their jobs—there is no reason why it should not be extended indefinitely, so that the structure of local government could be radically altered *within* the existing local government legislation. Indeed, Western Nigeria has been considering extending it, so that the important services of education, public health and works would be administered by much larger bodies than at present; though in the discussions that have taken place they have been thought of as 'service authorities', i.e. new authorities for the purpose of performing one function only—rather than as joint boards as at present constituted. The difference would be more than a mere difference in name, as certain constitutional and staffing changes are contemplated; but all this is still in the realm of speculation.

Enough has been said to illustrate the point that the areas of local government are capable of being constantly altered, and incidentally given different-sounding names, in order that a balance may be kept between the two aims of efficiency on the one hand and representative control on the other. It is all part of the changeable pattern of local government, but a warning needs to be given about rushing from one extreme to the other. Britain, as we have seen, has been too reluctant to alter her local government areas over a period of seventy or eighty years; but for West African countries to alter them too frequently could have an unsettling effect and might cause as much loss in efficiency as gain. Already there have been a number of major legislative changes in the first ten years, and councils and public alike have no sooner got used to one set of arrangements than they have had to learn to understand another; but this is probably a fault on the right side during the transitional period, while these new countries are finding out how much of the alien model is going to serve their needs, and how much ought to be altered. There is perhaps a case for a Standing Commission of high status, to keep the whole question under constant review, and to preserve a balance between stagnation on the one hand and too frequent disturbances on the other.

Before leaving this part of the subject, it is worth mentioning that there are some public services which can be provided both by small local authorities *and* by larger government agencies without necessarily coming into conflict, just as there can be a 'Concurrent List' of powers in the Constitution of Nigeria which permits both the Federal and the Regional governments to engage in the same activities. Water supplies are a very good example of this. One of the things which local authorities—even the smallest of them—can usefully do is to improve the supply of pure water, either by providing wells and standpipes, or by damming streams, keeping a clean access to them and filtering the water, as was done, for example, by the 'Henderson boxes' in use in Ghana. But equally the government can, in some parts of the country, sink bore holes or build bigger dams or reservoirs from which water can be pumped and piped over the area of several local authorities, by methods of engineering which would be beyond the resources even of a joint committee or board. There need be no conflict of interest here, since the demand for more and better water is almost unlimited; it is simply a question of which is the most appropriate body to provide it in different circumstances in which water can be found.

So far we have been considering functions which need to be performed over a wide geographical area in order to be efficient, but, as we said at the beginning of this chapter, there are some functions that could be performed satisfactorily in a *small* urban area, provided the council could afford to employ the necessary expert staff. But for the most part they cannot, and this brings us to the financial limitations within which they work. For example, the town of Port Harcourt in Nigeria, with a population of approximately 100,000, has a recurrent revenue of about £200,000; only about a quarter of that of a *municipal* borough, i.e. one with comparable powers, in Britain. Apart from government grants the revenues of local authorities depend on assessable property or income, and these are often very low indeed. It is true that there are some very wealthy people in West Africa, and that a small section of the population are large property owners, landlords, merchants or contractors; but they are a tiny section of the whole community, and the mass of people on whom local government depends for its finance are, from the rate collector's point of view, poor. We shall consider these questions more fully in the chapter on finance, but the immediate point is that some functions which are listed as local government functions in the laws cannot in fact be performed by local authorities because they lack the qualified staff. Two clear examples of this are town planning and housing.

The laws provide that Instruments may confer on local authorities a number of powers with regard to buildings, layouts, streets, plans, demolition and reconstruction which amount to what we call town planning; but even in the years since the original Local Government Ordinances were drafted the standards of professional and technical expertise required for modern town planning have grown enormously, new Town Planning Laws have been passed, and Town Planning Divisions have been created in appropriate ministries. Under these laws Town Planning Committees have been established which are not the same things as local councils, and which may be set up wherever the Minister deems it to be expedient. In Eastern Nigeria, for example, the planning authorities that have been created include only a small representation from the local councils—in one important town only the mayor and two other members—and in many ways the planning authority becomes a more influential body than the council. But the councils could not have begun to shoulder this responsibility since the councillors had no knowledge of the issues involved, and their staff could not possibly include the qualified architect, surveyor and draughtsmen that the town planning law rightly requires. The relationship between a planning authority and a council is in fact somewhat vague, and rests to some extent on the discretion of the chairman, who is usually the district officer. But there could be no question of the councils *being* the planning authorities, for the reasons given.

Again, according to the local government laws local authorities may in their Instruments be made housing authorities, but in fact most public housing, and all large-scale building of houses in estates, is undertaken by ministries or public corporations, who are the only agencies who can command the necessary resources of capital and skill.

Furthermore, although we speak of 'town' planning, really important planning cannot stop at the boundaries of a town. We have to consider the relationship between the town and the rural areas surrounding it, the best use to which certain areas of land should be put, the problems of transport and the movement of population. This is particularly so in a small and highly populated country like Britain, where every inch of land is used and where the phrase 'town and country planning' is normally employed; and where local authorities, although exercising planning powers, cannot be the *final* planning authorities, because their separate plans would overlap and conflict with one another; planning becomes a *national* responsibility. West African countries have not yet reached this stage, but even there it is impossible to separate the planning problems of a city from an overall plan for large areas surrounding the city.

The mere growth of towns is constantly posing problems

which are both technical, financial and political, for it leads to a situation where the statutory boundary ceases to correspond to the real boundary. Towns continually grow at their circumference, and as they do so urban services have constantly to be 'pushed out' in the area of other councils; eventually the town council wants to promote legislation for extending its statutory boundaries to correspond with the real facts, and this inevitably leads to opposition from the other affected councils, because not only do they dislike giving up some of their territory, but the part they are asked to give up is the most valuable from a revenue-producing point of view. This is a problem that can be seen on the outskirts of any growing town anywhere in the world, but it is particularly clearly illustrated in Lagos where the boundary between the Lagos town council (which is in Federal Territory) and the Western Region of Nigeria now runs through what is really one vast urban complex. The problem here also has political overtones, as the governments of the Federal Territory and the Western Region are in different political camps, so that if the boundaries of Lagos were extended not only would the Western Region lose a valuable revenue-producing area but the size of the Western Region would be diminished for the benefit of Federal Territory.

It is significant that in Northern Nigeria the present tendency is to elevate planning to be a *provincial* responsibility, a good example of a former local authority function being transferred to an authority of greater size.

The limitations of elected local councils are nowhere better seen than in the administration of large cities in West Africa. It is often said that the municipalities of West Africa correspond to the English county boroughs, but examination shows that this is far from being true, and that the functions of these councils are in fact somewhat restricted. This again is very clearly illustrated in the administration of Lagos, which admittedly has the complications of being both a Federal capital and the principal port.

The Lagos town council is a body of long standing, but until recently it was in essence a sanitary, public health and markets authority only; in the last few years it has acquired other responsibilities, notably a bus service purchased from private enterprise and the administration of primary education. But the town council, which operates on a budget of less than £1 million, could not possibly undertake responsibility for the major public services of the city. The Ministry of Lagos Affairs of the Federal Government is responsible for the major roads and streets and for the vital and expensive water supply; the Ports Authority is responsible for the city's most important undertaking; the Electricity Corporation supplies it with electricity; but above all a statutory corporation called the Lagos Executive Development Board, capitalized largely by the Federal Government and the Colonial Development Corporation, has been responsible for the huge undertaking of clearing the slums, replanning the city centre, and creating new housing estates on the outskirts. It has employed staff and equipment which would have been beyond the capacity of the town council, and has so far spent well over £10 million on capital projects.

Here we have an example of five different 'agencies', all *within* the same geographical area, performing functions best suited to the different kinds of work and to the resources which each can command. This is not necessarily a static situation; the area of responsibility of the town council is growing, and it is possible that as time goes by it may take over responsibilities both from the Federal Government and the Executive Development Corporation. This would be a matter of long-term policy, to which we shall return in the last chapter. Meanwhile, although the elected town council is represented on the other agencies, its own direct sphere of responsibility is restricted to what it can most competently do.

It may seem that some of the arguments of this chapter suggest that local government is not important. If government departments or agencies can do so many things better than elected local councils, why is so much thought and effort put into local government?

The key to the answer lies in representative or democratic control. In following the broad pattern and intention of British local government English-speaking West African countries have accepted the idea that as much government as possible should be locally controlled; that this will result in greater responsiveness to local needs and to the emergence of a healthy democratic society which produces responsible citizens. The logic of this is that every public service should be administered by the *smallest possible* unit. In the case of electricity this might be the whole country; in town and country planning, a province of the country; in education, a joint board of several local councils; but in a very wide range of services which are important to ordinary people it will be the local councils themselves, administering areas comparable to the present county, district, or local councils of Southern Nigeria and Ghana; these services are public health, public amenities, minor roads and works, markets and all other things which are by their nature *local*. The pattern may change; local authorities may need to become bigger, or they may have to lose some functions and acquire others; but nothing will ever destroy the need for local government, in any country in the world.

CHAPTER 8

Local Authorities and the Central Government

It is widely believed in West Africa today that local authorities are 'mere agents' of the central government. It is understandable that people should think this, but it was not the original intention, and if local councils had in the last ten years behaved more responsibly they would probably be enjoying greater freedom from central government control than they do today. To a very large extent, both in Britain and West Africa, they enjoy the freedom they deserve.

The relationship between central and local government in Britain, like that between councillors and officials, is one which Africans tend to find puzzling and unsatisfactory. They want a straightforward answer to the question 'Which is master and which is servant?', and are dissatisfied with the answer 'Neither'. In law the control of local authorities by the central government is considerable, though not as great as in West Africa; in practice the influence of unwritten conventions and personal relationships greatly modifies this fact.

Administrative control takes many forms in Britain. One of them is *inspection*; most people have heard of Her Majesty's Inspectors of Schools, whose duty is to see that local education authorities are properly fulfilling their responsibilities under the Education Act; there are also Home Office inspectors, who do the same for police forces, fire brigades, safety regulations, etc. The formal purpose of these inspectors is to see that services which Parliament has given to local authorities to administer, but which also have a national implication, and for which the Government pays grants-in-aid, are being maintained at a minimum level of efficiency; their informal purpose is to assist and advise; for inspection, like so many other things, is subject to unwritten conventions, and need not take the form, as is frequently supposed in West Africa, of finding fault and exacting retribution; an inspector may equally well be a friendly adviser.

Another form of control is by what are usually called *default powers*, which means that if a Minister is not satisfied with the way in which a local authority is performing its functions he may make an order requiring it to do certain things by a certain time, and if it fails to do so he may take the powers away from it and exercise them himself, either directly or by appointing a new authority to do so.

Again, certain matters which are within the general competence of local authorities nevertheless require *ministerial approval* before they are valid. Certain local authorities are responsible for building schools and houses; but they are required to submit the plans to the appropriate Ministry for approval, as the Government wants to make sure that certain standards are maintained throughout the country and that public funds are spent to the best advantage; for example, in the building of schools the Minister of Education will insist on certain *national*, not local, standards in such matters as design, space, ventilation, lighting, playgrounds, playing fields, equipment and so on. A more far-reaching control, but one on the other hand which throws great responsibilities on the local authority, is in the *submission of long-term schemes* to the Minister for development, e.g. in town and country planning and education.

Apart from these specific controls Ministers today have very considerable powers of *delegated legislation*. Most Acts of Parliament governing the services which local authorities administer deal only with broad principles; much of the detail is left to be filled in from time to time by 'the Minister', who is empowered under these Acts to make subsidiary legislation, in the form generally known as 'statuotry instruments'.

But alongside these controls of inspection, default powers, ministerial approval, submission of schemes and delegated legislation, there is constant consultation of a less formal kind between ministries and local authorities, both through demi-official correspondence and personal discussion between civil servants on the one hand and chief officers of local authorities, chairmen of committees and representative councillors on the other.

The fact that most local authorities behave responsibly means that controls are kept to a minimum and consultation to a maximum, and hence there can grow up a partnership between ministries and local authorities comparable to that between councillors and officials. Partnerships can of course vary in degree, and there can be senior, junior or equal partners; the kind of partnership which exists between government departments and local authorities varies with the subject matter. For example, in housing the Government could be called the senior partner, since it provides most of the money and keeps a close control on siting, design and cost; the local authority's function is to select the tenants and maintain the houses in good condition. In providing many local amenities, on the other hand, the local authority is the senior partner, for the Government is not heavily involved financially and does not wish to exercise control in the national interest. In education the partnership could be called an equal one, since the Ministry of Education keeps a tight control on the building, design, equipment and cost of schools, but the local authority has real independent responsibility for what happens inside them, in relation to children, teachers and syllabus.

But looking at the picture as a whole, British local authorities can justify their claim to be 'quasi-autonomous'. They do not have to submit their financial estimates for approval, they are given wide discretion in the award of contracts and the appointment of staff; some services they manage in their full discretion, and even in those which they manage under close government control they are a good deal more than agents. (It *is*, incidentally, possible for a local authority to act simply as an agent of a central government department, e.g. in the construction of national trunk roads through the area of a county council; but this is not an important aspect of their work, and incidentally has no relevance to West Africa, where county councils or their equivalents would not be competent to build trunk roads.)

Why, then, since the local government laws of West Africa set out to emulate British practice, is the idea so deeply rooted that local authorities are no more than the agents of government? The answer is that after allowing the new local authorities an initial burst of freedom, governments have increasingly tightened the controls which originally existed and have introduced new ones; and they have done this because the financial irresponsibility, bribery and corruption of councils compelled them to do it, and not because they wanted to. It is this which accounts for the three kinds of control which local authorities most resent, and which do not exist in the British system—approval of estimates, approval of the award of contracts (over a modest amount) and approval of the employment of staff. Such controls need not, however, be permanent. One very significant event has taken place in recent years in Western Nigeria, where the Government has decided to grant 'financial autonomy' to those councils which have earned it by a good financial record, including a record of rate collection, over a period of years. This frees them from most government financial controls, though not of course from government audit.

The controls which we have outlined above as being characteristic of British local government can of course all be found in the West African local government laws, or alternatively in subsidiary (delegated) legislation or administrative instructions. So far as the principal laws are concerned they are most fully and explicitly set out in the Eastern Nigerian Law (Part III—'Powers of the Minister') and the Western Nigerian Law (Part XI—'General Powers of Supervision and Inspection'). The Ghana Local Government Act of 1961 includes most of the same provisions, but is arranged rather differently. In the first place the Minister has wide powers to amend the Instrument establishing a council, though he can only exercise this power after giving the council concerned an opportunity to express its views, and after obtaining the approval of the President; this power allows him to alter the council's functions and even gives him a considerable say in its internal arrangements. He may also alter the area of a local authority, though in this case only after a public enquiry has been held. There is no counterpart to these particular controls in British local government, because the councils do not have individual Instruments—every council of a given status exercises the same functions, and alterations of this order would need legislation by Parliament.

The remaining powers of the Minister, in all three countries, are more familiar to British local government, from which indeed they were originally copied, and are largely concerned with councils which fail in their duties or responsibilities, i.e. they are default powers. Thus if a council fails to hold regular meetings, or is not using its revenues in a responsible way, or is manifestly corrupt, or is failing to levy and collect the rates, the Minister may dissolve it and either establish a new one or appoint some other 'fit and proper persons, not being less than five in number', to take their place; these have come to be known generally as 'caretaker committees'. In Western Nigeria a single person, called a 'sole administrator', has more than once been appointed instead of a committee of management, to use the more formal name. Such measures apply if there is a *general* failure on the part of the council to carry out its responsibilities, but another provision of the law entitles the Minister to take action if a council is failing simply in one particular duty, or if it is failing to make and enforce by-laws with consequent 'danger to the health, safety or welfare of the public'; in such cases he may issue an instruction requiring it to take the necessary action, and if it fails to do so he may cause it to be taken by other means. Finally the Minister has an important general power to hold enquiries, at his own discretion, into the affairs of any council.

These controls sound very drastic, and may give the impression that local councils are entirely 'under the thumb' of the Minister. There is, however, nothing unusual in their existence, and any council in Britain which failed to carry out its responsibilities would be subject to similar discipline. What is unusual, and deplorable, is that experience has made it necessary to give such disciplinary controls a prominent place in the law, and to exercise them fairly frequently. But this has arisen from a failure in the human element, and cannot be held as a criticism of the local government laws or of the institution of local government.

There is another important control, which will be found in any local government system in the world, namely *audit*. The accounts of local authorities must be audited by persons appointed by the Minister (usually the Government Auditor and his staff), and the auditors must consider not only the accuracy of the accounting but the legality of all expenditure; here we return to the legal doctrine of *ultra vires*, by which local authorities may only do those things which the law says they may do. If they spend money on a purpose which is not specified in their Instrument the auditors may disallow such expenditure, and the person or persons responsible for it may be 'surcharged' with the amount—that is, they may be compelled to pay it back out of their own pockets. The Eastern Nigerian Government has recently been enforcing this provision rather strictly, with the result that a large number of councillors (with whom the responsibility usually rests) have had to make substantial repayments, thus providing a very healthy check on corruption.

One of the most regrettable things about local government in West Africa, ever since its reorganization in the early 1950's, has been that the Government Auditors' offices have been understaffed and overworked, and have not been able to give the assistance to local council treasurers that they would have liked. For an auditor need not necessarily be an inspector whose arrival is dreaded, and who comes to find fault; indeed Government auditors would much rather play the role of teachers and helpers of local council treasurers; and treasurers, many of whom have had scant training for their work, would welcome such expert guidance; both sides would much prefer prevention to cure (or punishment). But such is the pressure on the auditors that they have frequently been more than a year behindhand with their work, so that they have only been able to study the accounts after mistakes or illegalities have been committed, and they have not been able to spend enough time at the councils' headquarters to act as teachers or advisers.

Fortunately all the governments we are considering have been making efforts in recent years to supplement the work of the Audit Department by training their own executive officers in this specialized work. In Eastern Nigeria an 'Examination of Accounts' Division has been created in the Ministry of Local Government, and in both Nigerian Regions executive officers are attached to Provincial Offices, or to Local Government Advisers, for the special purpose of carrying out frequent checks on the local authorities' accounts, conducting internal audits, and advising and training local council treasurers on the spot. This work has been given a high priority, and not only has it increased financial efficiency, but it has greatly assisted the Audit Departments. The way in which the problem has been tackled in Ghana is mentioned later in this chapter (p. 105).

This is an appropriate point at which to introduce a wider topic—that of inspection and advice generally. Since the early 1950's local authorities have been called upon to undertake responsibilities of a kind which require maturity and experience, and to perform unfamiliar functions under complicated laws and regulations. It would have been reasonable, in these early years, to give them close inspection and support. Unfortunately these years have coincided with the withdrawal, or at least the diminution, of control by the district officer or district commissioner; this arose partly from deliberate policy, and partly from a progressive shortage of administrative officers, caused to some extent by the departure of expatriates. The point is worth discussing a little more fully.

In the days of the native authorities 'Divisions' or 'Districts' (the name varied) were effectively administered by the DO (or DC), who was the local representative of the central government and its principal agent. NAs were slowly acquiring greater responsibilities, as they showed themselves fit for them, but the DO was the 'power in the land', and NAs which were irresponsible, corrupt or inefficient could be effectively checked or controlled by him. The transition to 'local government', especially a system of local government modelled so closely on the British pattern, raised difficult questions of principle. In the first place, there was no one in the British system who corresponded to the DO—indeed, a local representative of the Government, exercising comprehensive powers, would be foreign and repugnant to British local government; secondly, it was the general intention that local authorities should *replace* the DO, and that elected representatives of the people should take over the control of local affairs which he previously exercised.

For this reason among others administrative officers in Southern Nigeria have never had the same control over the county, divisional or district councils that they used to have over the native authorities. The Residents, and the system of provincial administration, were abolished quite suddenly, for reasons that were partly rational but largely emotional. It is true that the growth of a ministerial system of government, and the shrinking of the size of the country because of improved communications, had greatly altered the functions of a Resident, and in the more developed areas, especially near the capital cities, had diminished them; though the work of Residents in the more inaccessible and backward provinces had not noticeably altered. Possibly more important, however, was that the Resident, more than any other official, represented colonial rule, and his continued existence was unacceptable to the new governments. Whatever the reasons, it is clear in retrospect that little thought was given to the purpose which the Resident had served in the past, and that he might serve in the future, simply in terms of the efficient administration of a country like Southern Nigeria. It would have been interesting, and might have influenced later policy, if someone had tried to compare the place of the Resident in Provincial Nigeria with that of the Prefect in Provincial France; there are some similarities, both in principle and detail, between the two offices, and now, ten years later, many people are saying that Nigeria has much to learn from France about provincial and local government; had the Residents, or a majority of them, been Nigerians instead of expatriates it is possible that they would have remained.

It was, however, the DO rather than the Resident himself who had supervised the native authorities, and what happened to him varied a good deal. In Eastern Nigeria his title has survived and his duties are now much what they have always been. But in the vital years of 1950–5 his powers in relation to local government were virtually abolished; he had literally no legal rights beyond the right to inspect the books if he had reason to believe there was irregularity; and having inspected them he had no power to do more than make a report to the Ministry. It was during these five years, when the control of local authorities should have been close, that it became non-existent, and it was then that bribery, corruption and nepotism got a firm hold in local government. An Ordinance of 1955 and an Act of 1960 reversed this trend and greatly strengthened the Minister's control of the councils, which he exercised largely through the district officers. In Eastern Nigeria, therefore, the DO's position has swung back to what it used to be.

In Western Nigeria, by contrast, it has weakened. The title was abolished and replaced by that of 'Local Government Adviser', an unsatisfactory title in that many of his duties have nothing to do with local government, and that local authorities do not take his advice. Moreover, government administrative areas have been enlarged and LGAs have to administer impossibly large areas; there are at the time of writing twenty-one LGAs and Assistant LGAs compared with seventy-four DOs and ADOs in 1954. Ministerial control of the authorities is, as we have said, powerful, and must be exercised largely through the LGAs, but they lack the inherent authority of the former DO and cannot control councils in which party politics are paramount.

The situation in Ghana is different again, because administrative control by local agents of the central government, though not by the old 'all-purpose' District Commissioner, has in the long run been strengthened. The title of DC gave way to that of 'Government Agent', a simple and descriptive one which had much to commend it. Although Government Agents had no statutory duties under the old local government Ordinance, supervision of local authorities was a recognized part of their duties,[1] and there was no sudden change. However, they have now ceased to exist, and the title of 'District Commissioner' has been revived to describe a political and not an administrative appointment. What has taken their place, however, is a local government inspectorate, consisting of an administrative officer at each Regional headquarters,[2] served by small teams of inspectors responsible for groups of local authorities. Their duties are specific, and include a close supervision of the accounts and the performance of the authorities. This trend in Ghana is significant, because it recognizes the fact that elected local authorities, in a country at Ghana's stage of development, cannot reasonably be expected to assume, in a short period of years, the full responsibilities of local administration without central control and guidance.

Indeed, it is clear from the experiences of all three countries that this is so.

What is becoming apparent, however, is that it is no longer the *intention* that local representatives of the central government shall disappear. In Eastern Nigeria and Ghana

---

[1] 'Ten Years of Local Government in Ghana': A. F. Greenwood: *Journal of Local Administration Overseas*, January 1962.

[2] There are eight Regions, and the word is roughly comparable to the Nigerian 'Province'.

(and incidentally in Northern Nigeria and Sierra Leone, with which we will deal later) the former Residents (Nigeria) and Provincial Commissioners (Ghana), who were civil servants, have been replaced by commissioners who are not; they are in fact politicians who in Ghana, Northern Nigeria and Sierra Leone have the status of Minister. Alongside them in Nigeria are civil servants, known as Provincial Secretaries, and behind them elected Provincial Assemblies.

This has not, however, happened in Western Nigeria at the time of writing.

These developments may come to have a profound effect on local government. The relationship between the Provincial Commissioner and the Provincial Secretary is similar to that between a Minister and his Permanent Secretary. The Provincial Commissioner has no direct statutory control over the local authorities, since his function is the much wider one of bringing the Government into closer touch with the people, explaining its policies and endeavouring to see that they are implemented; the dividing line between 'Government' and 'Party' is not, of course, always very clear-cut. The Provincial Secretary, on the other hand, has definite responsibilities for the local authorities—indeed in Eastern Nigeria he is in one of his capacities 'commissioner for local government', and in Northern Nigeria his responsibilities are equally specific. From this, combined with his relationship to the Provincial Commissioner, it follows that Commissioner and Secretary alike may influence the future of local government very considerably.

This represents a trend opposite to that of ten years ago, when a more representative system of local government was first launched. What we see happening is a reversion to provincial (or in Ghana regional) authorities, with the important difference that the head of the Province is a nominee of the party in power and not a civil servant. This cannot be without its effect on local government in the long run, because the Provincial Commissioner and his office could be said to be a form of 'local government' in themselves—a projection of the central government into the provinces. In other words, two of the concepts of local government which we discussed in the first chapter are emerging side by side in Eastern and Northern Nigeria, Ghana and Sierra Leone; while in Western Nigeria there is at the time of writing an uneasy pause; the structure of local government is statutorily unchanged from five years ago and there has been no systematic revival of provincial administration; on the other hand changes are undoubtedly impending, and it will be a matter of great interest to see what the next developments are.

All that has been said in the last few pages emphasizes the point which was made in the first chapter—that these countries, needing a new point of departure, took British local government as a provisional model; that ten years have now been spent in modifying it to suit local circumstances, and in learning by trial and error; that new trends, deriving from African and not from British experience, have become embodied in the local government laws; and that a new pattern of national-provincial-local government is falling into place. But it will be another ten years before any writer will be able to describe with confidence what the local government system is like, in any enduring sense.

CHAPTER 9

The Revenue of Local Authorities

THE chapter on the Work of Local Authorities gave an approximate idea of how local authorities *spend* their money. It is impossible, unfortunately, to make any useful generalizations which would apply to Eastern and Western Nigeria and Ghana, because the share of the work undertaken by central and local authorities is not always comparable. Thus in a recent year Education accounted for 56 per cent of expenditure by local authorities in Western Nigeria, but only 32 per cent in the East. On the other hand expenditure on Works was 27 per cent in the East and only 13 per cent in the West, and on Health 13 per cent in the East and 7 per cent in the West. This does not necessarily mean that certain services are being neglected; it may only mean that they are being provided in different ways. All that one can say is that education, works and health services absorb most of the local authorities' money, with the cost of overhead administration running at a little under 15 per cent of the total expenditure.

When we turn to the question of how they *get* their money it is equally difficult to generalize. The two principal sources of revenue are government grants and local rates; but even here the proportion of the former varied recently from 52 per cent of the authorities' total revenue in Eastern Nigeria to only about 40 per cent in Western Nigeria and Ghana; local rates were represented by 27 per cent in Eastern Nigeria, but 44 per cent in the West. However, these two sources of revenue are between them much more important than any other, and we will now consider them in turn.

GOVERNMENT GRANTS

The relationship between central and local government, which we discussed in the last chapter, is really defined in the financial grant aid which local authorities receive from the central government. For why do governments give grant aid to local authorities at all? Obviously the work in question has to be done, but the fact that the Government aids the local authorities in this way signifies two things; first, that they think it will be better provided through the agency of a locally elected council, with some local independence, rather than through their own departmental organization; secondly, and in apparent contradiction to this, they want to exercise some control over the council so that they can see that the work is done properly in the national as well as in the local interest.

Grant aid can be given in several ways, but there are two principal ones. First it may be a *percentage* of what the service is going to cost. The percentage type of grant may be illustrated from current practice in Western Nigeria.

This is an area, it will be recalled, where there are local government police forces, and in order to assist councils to maintain them, and also to give the Government a right to inspect them, the Government pays for 50 per cent of their recurrent costs; they also pay 25 per cent of their capital costs, that is the cost of such things as new buildings and equipment, as distinct from pay and annual upkeep. The health services for which the local authorities are responsible, on the other hand, receive only 10 per cent, recurrent and capital. It could be argued, though this is speculative, that these facts indicate that the Government regard the maintenance of law and order as having a greater national significance than the local sanitary services and dispensaries. This principle can certainly be seen in the grants for the upkeep of roads, for these vary from nil for local laterite roads to £84 per mile for the most important 'provincial' roads, with many graduations in between; the wider the use to which the road is put the greater the percentage grant. The same principle may be seen, though applied in a slightly different way, in the service which is regarded as being the most important of all, namely education; for here the Government pays 100 per cent of the salaries of primary school teachers, local education officers, supervising teachers and their essential staff, leaving the local authorities themselves to bear the cost of maintaining the schools in good repair. It is interesting, incidentally, that in this Region, which has a 'unified local government service' for certain grades, the Government pays 50 per cent of their salaries. To take a quite different kind of example, this is a Region which in its coastal areas relies a good deal on waterways for transport, and the Government pays 50 per cent of the cost of keeping them navigable.

This system of percentage grants is universal, and the example of Western Nigeria has been used merely to give it a little local colour. It is not, however, without its problems, and the trend in Britain at the moment is away from percentage grants, and towards a different kind of grant which we will discuss in a moment. Its worst defect is that it tends to help the rich authorities proportionately more than the poorer ones. In private life, if someone offers you £1 for £1 to help you to buy a car, his offer will not help you to buy a very good car if you can only scrape together £100 yourself. Similarly, an offer of 50 per cent grant aid for a certain service will help richer authorities to provide a very good service but will still impose a limit on what can be done in a poorer area, where the service may be much more greatly needed.

To overcome this defect, governments in Britain and other countries have devised what are called 'equalization' grants, designed to give a higher proportion of aid to those authorities which are naturally poor than to those which are naturally rich. This type of grant in Britain was started thirty years ago in circumstances which are not relevant to this discussion; indeed, they have now greatly altered, and the method of calculating the grant has several times been changed. But the principle remains. There are certain areas which because of their past history or their local natural resources are worse off financially than others, and it is just in these places, which can least afford them, that expensive social services are most needed. To meet this difficulty a formula was devised which took into account the main factors which held back development and which caused expensive services to be needed. These factors were the rate of local unemployment, the proportion of children to adults in the population (since children are the cause of some of the most expensive services), the way in which the value of property in the council's area compared with the average for the whole country, and the degree to which the area of the authority was scattered or compact, since distances are one of the factors which add to expense; this last calculation, incidentally, was made on the basis of 'population per road mile'.

It is obvious that a calculation of this kind is a very complicated one, which could not be made without a tremendous volume of reliable statistical information. This is important from the West African point of view, because the same problem of natural inequality is at least as great there as in Britain. Some authorities are, for example, in wealthy cocoa-growing areas, where the general level of prosperity is high; others may be in semi-desert areas where people exist on their cattle and a little subsistence agriculture, or, by contrast, in crowded towns with heavy unemployment and a serious lack of urban social services. From the point of view of national equality some should receive more grant aid from the Government than others, and a straightforward percentage grant, while naturally helping everybody, might make the actual disparity between rich and poor greater instead of less. Unfortunately the statistical information which is needed to devise a fair equalization grant is still very largely lacking in West Africa, and equalization grants, though accepted in principle, have to be based on very crude calculations, usually the simple one of the estimated relative population of the different authorities.

The Federal Government of Nigeria faces a similar problem in devising how the Federal revenue derived from import and export duties shall be distributed to the Regions on the principle of 'need', as distinct from that of 'derivation'. The principle of need means that a certain proportion of this revenue is paid to the Regions not because the produce was exported from them, or because the imported goods are being purchased by them, but because one Region is in greater need than another from natural causes. Here is a very comparable situation, on the national level, where an equalization formula is necessary; but the calculation can only be based on two factors, both rather 'rough and ready', the estimated population and the estimated income per head.

Reverting to percentage grants, their other weakness is that they detract from the independence of local authorities to spend their money in the way they think fit. If most of the grant revenue is in the form of percentage aid for specific services their policy of development is very largely dictated for them, except in relatively minor matters in which they find all the money themselves; in which case they are indeed in danger of becoming 'mere agents' of the Government. It is this argument which has recently caused the Government of Britain to abolish most percentage grants in favour of grants which amount to very much the same in total, but which can be spent more at the discretion of the local councils, a decision which has provoked a great deal of controversy. However, there has always been controversy about the relative merits of percentage grants and the other kind of grant (usually called the 'block' grant) which has 'no strings attached', and policy has leaned now in one direction and now in another. The percentage grant is likely to be of particular value in an undeveloped country, because it is useful for getting new services started—services which may be unpopular or little understood, and which would have little chance of being developed if they had to depend entirely on local initiative; the block grant is more suitable for assisting a responsible and well-developed authority to keep its services going.

However, block grants are already established in West

Africa alongside percentage grants, and in Eastern Nigeria, apart from a special education grant, it is now the principal method by which the Government assists local authorities.

There are no fixed rules about the ways in which grant aid may be given, but simply certain well-established practices. Percentage grants and block grants have been discussed in a little detail because they are the most usual, but governments may make any variations that may seem to them expedient in different circumstances. Many grants are of a special or *ad hoc* kind, given once and for all for a particular purpose, especially for capital expenditure. For example, Western Nigeria gives local authorities 40 per cent of the cost of rural health centres, 50 per cent of urban water supplies and 100 per cent for rural water supplies, but the arrangements for maintaining these services vary considerably; in the case of urban water supplies the Government give a subsidy which will keep the local water rate below a certain figure which it is believed the inhabitants can afford.

There is accordingly room for infinite variety in the matter of Government grants, and the important thing is not so much to learn precisely how they are awarded at any particular time and place, because this is constantly changing, but to appreciate the principles which govern their award.

LOCAL RATES

Although local authorities receive some 40–50 per cent of their revenue from Government grants, and although there are good reasons why this should be so, it is obvious that if local government is going to have any real meaning the authorities must be able to raise a comparable amount from their own resources, which of course they do. The most important item of this 'home-produced' revenue is the local rate, which is a form of local tax on individuals, on income or on property; in certain cases, such as an education or water rate, it is a payment for a specific service.

Unfortunately the local rate, when it is levied upon individuals or their incomes as distinct from their property, is apt to become entangled with the central income tax assessed and collected by the Inland Revenue Department or its equivalent, and it is not always easy to disentangle the two. It is certainly impossible to make a brief general statement which will cover all three countries, as their history and present practice in this respect vary so much. It was the general practice in colonial days for the native authorities to collect the tax (there being only one kind of tax) and for the proceeds to be divided between the Government and the native authority, each taking a fixed percentage. Often this arrangement worked well for the native authorities, who were allowed to keep a high proportion, and sometimes the whole, but the proportion was inclined to vary according to the financial pressures on the governments at any given time, and the whole tax belonged in principle to the governments; as people became wealthier, and the assessment of a *graduated* tax became more complicated, it was clear that the native authorities, and the local authorities which succeeded them, were not really as competent to work a system of graduated income tax as they had been to collect the 'flat' tax of earlier days; too much was required in the way of staff, information and office organization. Accordingly income tax departments grew up in the central governments for the purpose of collecting a tax from people of easily ascertainable incomes, or from traders and merchants who moved from place to place, or from expatriates, or from commercial firms, or from others for whom the simple apparatus of the local authority's tax office was inappropriate. Broadly speaking income tax would go to the Government and local rates to the local authority, but unfortunately the actual position is not as simple as this. In Western Nigeria the local authorities still collect income tax from the great majority of individual taxpayers (though not the special, and wealthier, categories) but are allowed by the Government to retain the whole of it. In Eastern Nigeria the central government became the taxing authority in 1956, and for some years afterwards the local rate, imposed in addition, had to be kept down by the Government in order not to prejudice the collection of income tax (though this restraint has now been relaxed). In Ghana the position is that the machinery of central government income tax is gradually working downwards, as it becomes easier to ascertain more and more individual incomes, and as the techniques of assessment and collection improve. Generally speaking, the two systems try to 'keep out of each other's way' as much as possible, but as the laws stand it is often possible for a man to be liable for the same *kind* of tax from two different sources. It will probably be some years before a permanent relationship between the two is settled.[1]

Meanwhile, however, the Instruments of all the major local authorities declare them to be 'rating authorities',[2] and give them not only the power to levy rates but the positive duty to collect sufficient rates for the services which they budget to provide. There are several ways in which they may do this, which are set out in great detail in the local government laws of Southern Nigeria and Ghana; it is not easy to summarize these laws, since they differ in their arrangement and there are indeed some differences in substance between them. With variations, however, they allow councils to impose rates in the following ways:

A capitation rate

This is the oldest form of rating in these countries, dating from early colonial days, and it used to be called by such names as 'head' or 'poll' tax. It is now generally regarded as an archaic form of taxation, but provision is still made for it, since there are still many people who ought to be taxed but whose income is small and not easily ascertainable. In Nigeria it may be imposed on people over sixteen years of age and in Ghana over eighteen. In Western Nigeria the assumption is made that everybody who appears to be taxable must have a minimum income of £50 p.a., and the capitation rate

[1] For an excellent study of this whole subject, which it is impossible to summarize here, see G. Oka Orewa: *Taxation in Western Nigeria*, NISER—OUP, 1962.

[2] Excluding the small so-called 'local councils' which form the lowest tier of the structure in Eastern and Western Nigeria.

is fixed at £1 17s 6d; in Eastern Nigeria it was reduced to 5s some years ago, when the Government took over responsibility for central taxation, but it has since gone on rising and the average capitation rate is now about £1. But although it remains, and will be a valuable source of revenue for some time to come, it is more and more giving way to the second form of local rating, i.e.

A rate on assessable income

This gets away from the unsatisfactory principle of everyone paying the same and introduces the principle of paying what they can afford on a graduated scale, and it is quite simply a form of local income tax. It is assessed by local assessment committees of the councils, an arrangement which has some unsatisfactory features, being among other things extremely open to corruption, though in Western Nigeria, for example, this is being improved because of the advice and supervision given by the Regional Tax Board. The principle of a graduated tax is sound, though as countries develop local rates on income are probably more appropriate to rural than to urban areas, which are likely to rely more and more on rates on fixed property.

These rates on individuals are intended for the general revenue of the councils, to enable them to meet a wide range of commitments. But it is also possible to levy on individuals

A Special Rate

This expression can have two meanings:

(*a*) It can mean a rate levied upon everybody in a council area for a special purpose, such as a school or a water supply (to name the two most usual). In Britain rates of this kind have largely died away, because it is simpler and cheaper to collect one consolidated rate, and people who like to know how their money is being spent can always learn, because the facts are printed on the rate demand note in very great detail. But this cannot yet be done in West Africa, and although no one in any country enjoys paying his rates it has been found from experience that the special rate is popular, or at any rate people object to paying it less than they do the general rate. This is a point of some importance among unsophisticated people; they resent having to pay a rate for the general purposes of the council, because they cannot understand what happens to the money and are suspicious—sometimes rightly—that it will be wasted; but if they are told that in return for paying a special rate they will get a school or a standpipe they will pay willingly. Like all of us they like to see something for their money.

(*b*) It can also mean a rate levied upon people living in certain parts of a local authority area, and not over the whole area. This is especially appropriate in rural areas, where a service may be provided in part of the area but not the whole. If a certain village is provided by the council with a supply of piped water, people in another village ten miles away who are still carrying buckets to a stream will not be enthusiastic about paying for it, even if they do happen to be in the same council area.

A Rate on Property

This is an increasingly important kind of rate, especially in urban areas. Property means in effect buildings, whether they are dwelling houses, offices, shops, cinemas or indeed almost any kind of premises, though the Ghana Act does in fact permit a rate to be assessed on 'possessions, or any category of possessions'.

Rates on property are the basis of local taxation in more developed countries, and especially in Britain where there are no rates on local income. Although like any form of taxation they occasionally give rise to anomalies and injustices, they are thought to be the best basis for local rating, chiefly because the revenue derived from them is permanent, dependable and forseeable. They are based on the idea that the owner (or in the case of dwelling houses it may be the owner or occupier) should pay a rate which is related to the value of his property. There are several alternative ways of assessing what this value is, and different countries use different systems. In Britain valuation is based on a calculation of what rent the property would command if it were let. In Ghana it is the estimated capital value of the property; for example, if a house is thought to be worth £500, allowance having been made for depreciation, a rateable value would be calculated from this and a rate of the order of 6d or 1s in the £ charged upon it; if the calculation were based on 10 per cent of the capital value the rate would accordingly be 25s or 50s. To take an example from Eastern Nigeria, a larger and better type of house might be valued at £2,000 and under the formula in use in that Region its rateable value might be assessed at £100 p.a.; a customary rate at the time of writing could well be 2s in the £, which would make the owner liable to an annual rate of £10. In Sierra Leone there is a simpler calculation; houses made of mud and wattle with a thatch or bamboo roof are valued at £1 per room per annum; a corrugated iron roof and mud blocks would send it up to £3 per room; concrete or timber walls to £5 or £10, according to the construction of the roof; the current rate levied by town councils is 3s in the £, so that a two-roomed house in the lowest category would pay 3s in the £ on £2, i.e. 6s; whereas a four-roomed house in the higest category would pay 3s on £40, i.e. £6. Business premises are usually rated as so much per square foot, according to the purpose of the building and its locality in the town, a principle which can also be applied to dwelling houses.

The possible variations are enormous, and the whole question of property rating is a highly specialized study. Even the process of valuing property for rating purposes requires expert knowledge, as is shown by the fact that in Ghana experts have been recruited from the United Nations Technical Assistance Organization to train Ghanaian valuers; the valuation of Freetown for property rating occupied a large team of valuers over five years.

Property rating has not made very much headway yet in West Africa, but it is spreading at an accelerating pace. In Ghana 'it is becoming increasingly popular and its further development is only limited by the number of valuers available to assess the property.'[1] In Eastern Nigeria it operates in the eight largest towns, and the valuation is made by the local councils, with guiding rules supplied by the Government valuer. In Western Nigeria it has made surprisingly little headway, and is confined to the three towns of Sapele, Warri and Abeokuta, and even the capital city of Ibadan has no property rating, but depends on personal capitaton and income rates.[2] In Sierra Leone it is being applied in a few of the main 'townships' in addition to Freetown, the valuation being done by leading members of the town councils.

We must leave the subject of rating here, although it requires a book to itself. There is space only for two general comments. First, the various kinds of rates which we have just outlined may give the impression that local government may well cost the individual a small fortune, especially when it is remembered that personal *and* property rates may be levied at the same time; the question arises of what it is reasonable that a man should pay to his local council for local services. Very little research has been done into what he actually does pay in relation to his total income. In Britain, at a very rough calculation, the ordinary man living in a council house might pay about two weeks' wages in the year in local rates, but he gets a good deal more in return for his money than most Africans; some recent calculations in Western Nigeria proceeded on the basis that 5 per cent of income 'to the public purse' would be reasonable, whereas in Ghana the yardstick used by local authorities was 1 per cent of assessable income for *local* tax, subject to an upward limit of £5. Everything turns, of course, on 'value for money'; people will pay cheerfully if they see results and will try to evade their obligations if they don't. This leads to the second point, that throughout West Africa in town and 'bush' alike, arrears of rates are an unceasing and apparently insoluble problem. 'Tax drives' are constantly being used to get in as much as possible in order to avoid financial crises, but

---

[1] A. F. Greenwood, *Journal of Local Administration Overseas*, op. cit.
[2] The Ibadan City Council has now adopted property rating in principle.

nowhere are the general rates paid regularly, promptly and without trouble. This, we must hope, is a matter of education, and that it will improve as understanding of public affairs develops, but few people at the moment seem able to realize the effects of rate arrears, in the non-payment of salaries and the suspension of public services.

A little more needs to be said about the assessment, or the calculation of the amount, of the rate. In the case of capitation or income rates this means calculating how much each individual shall pay, and this, as we have said, is usually done by local assessment committees; in the case of property rating it means deciding how many shillings and pence in the £ shall be charged on the annual value of the property, however this may be determined. The actual *valuation* is sometimes done by the Inland Revenue Department of the Government (which is now the British practice) and sometimes by a committee of the councils themselves (which used to be the British practice, but which was abandoned in order to get greater national uniformity). But the *assessment* is done by the local authorities themselves, in their capacity of rating authorities, and it is one of their most important responsibilities. It must be remembered, however, that councils' estimates (with the exception of a few 'financially autonomous' councils in Western Nigeria) are subject to the approval of the Government, and in practice governments have often had to restrain councils from making a rate which they (the governments) thought unreasonably high, and have tried to establish a more or less uniform level of assessment throughout the country. This is especially true of personal, as distinct from property, rating in the rural areas, where councils in the first flush of enthusiasm, and in their desire to create improvements in their area, often overestimated the ratepayers' willingness, or even ability, to pay.

In spite of the restraining arm of government, however, the annual fixing of the rate is an important event in the work of any council, and it is necessary to understand how they set about it, for there is a change here from the old days of native administration. The NA used to sit down once a year and decide what the tax ought to be, i.e. how much people could afford to pay; having added up what this would come to they then worked out how much they could afford to spend, and what to spend it on. Local authorities today adopt the more progressive approach of first working out what they want and how much it would cost; they then consider the total value of the property which is subject to rating, or the incomes of the people subject to income rating, and the number of people subject to capitation rating, and then work out what the rate would have to be fixed at if they were to be able to do what they wanted. Of course they are limited by what is possible and they generally finish by having to 'cut their coat according to their cloth', but there is none the less a very important difference in the two approaches to the problem. It should be added that there is provision in all the laws for ratepayers to appeal against their assessment, for certain people, e.g. the old or infirm, to be exempted from rating, and for certain kinds of property, e.g. churches or community centres, to receive preferential assessment.

MINOR SOURCES OF REVENUE

Grants and rates account between them for more than 80 per cent of the revenue of local authorities, but there remains 20 per cent or so which comes from other sources, and this is not an inconsiderable amount. It is raised in miscellaneous ways.

A large proportion of it may come from the administration of the local courts, in fines and fees, though the expenses of the court have to be set against this and it is quite possible for there to be a deficit instead of a surplus. It is not a good principle that the revenue of the courts should come to be relied on as income for local government, and it is something of an anomaly that while the personnel of the courts has been separated from that of the councils their finances are still so closely intertwined. Obviously the local authorities must be reimbursed for the cost of maintaining the courts, which is one of their statutory duties, but the principle of financing local services from the profits of crime is open to question and could lead to abuses.

Another source of revenue is from fees charged for specific services, which ought to be paid for by the individuals who use them rather than by the whole community in the form of rates. Examples are the fees for car or lorry parks, for the use of slaughter houses or for market stalls (although these could more properly be called rents). These, however, should not be regarded as a significant source of revenue, as the real purpose of charging fees is to defray the cost of providing the service, e.g. paying the wages of supervisors, attendants or cleaners; in principle the object should be to provide the service at the lowest cost rather than to think of it as a source of general revenue. The same principle should apply to the larger undertakings of the big cities e.g. the fares charged for a municipal bus service should be as low as is consistent with maintaining and improving the service and setting aside enough money for depreciation and replacements; some bus services can be highly profitable, and there is a temptation for the authority to regard them as a source of revenue for general purposes instead of a service to the people who use them.

Then there are various kinds of 'licences', which may be for such varied purposes as bicycles, carts, canoes, palm-wine shops, bakeries, slaughter houses, firearms, drumming or entertainments. Here again there is apt to be a confusion of principle. The purpose of making people take out licences ought to be either because it is undesirable to have too many of a certain thing, e.g. palm-wine sellers or hawkers; or because there is something potentially dangerous or insanitary which ought to be inspected and controlled, like firearms on the one hand or bakeries and slaughter houses on the other. While it is convenient to treat these as sources of income there needs to be a sense of moderation. There is a temptation to want to licence, for the sake of the fees, certain things which are really helping to develop the country, and which ought to be encouraged rather than taxed. In countries with very little public transport bicycles are an advantage, as are any forms of vehicle which can replace the inefficient system of head-loading. The licencing principle, when applied to these, is more open to question, for it may amount to a tax on progress.

Lastly, some local authorities, though by no means all, derive revenue from such things as the sale of timber or firewood from forest reserves, local industries such as weaving and pottery, and the profits of seed nurseries or agricultural plots; while the larger urban authorities often earn a considerable revenue from rents and leases.

Nevertheless it is the general and special rate, backed by central government grants, which is the foundation of local authority revenue.

LOANS

So far we have spoken almost entirely in terms of the recurrent revenue which councils need for their work, though we mentioned in passing that Government grants may include grants for capital expenditure. But major capital developments cannot be financed in this way, and councils which aspire to more ambitious schemes, such as a large-scale market development, a drainage scheme or a town hall would normally try to raise a loan, the interest and capital of which would be repaid over a long period of years. Here again there has been a significant change from the old days of native administration, for NAs were not allowed to borrow, and if they wanted to spend money they first had to save it little by little out of annual surpluses (which were obligatory); this obviously held back development. It has since been realized that borrowing, subject of course to adequate security for the loan, offers the only way to make progress. It is also more equitable than paying for large capital projects out of savings, for the people who will enjoy the benefits of the project are the coming generations, who can reasonable be expected to pay for it out of the rates that they will pay in future years.

The sections of the local government laws which deal with

borrowing are almost identical. Councils may raise loans, subject to the prior approval of the Minister, from any proper source within the country—the Government itself, the banks or public corporations established for the purpose; the security for the loan is 'the property and revenues of the council', and there are naturally stringent provisions in the law about councils which default on the payment of interest or capital. The extent to which loans can be raised is of course limited by the amount of loan capital which is available in the country and by the credit-worthiness of the councils, and compared with Britain, where in 1959–60 the local authorities raised the astonishing sum of £513,495,000 in loans for capital development, progress has been modest; nevertheless a good many useful projects of the kind mentioned have been financed by loans of the order of £100,000, which means that progress has been made which could never have been made in the days when native authorities had to save before they could spend. If the projects themselves are revenue-producing, like a big market or a bus service, or in the longer term like a drainage scheme or a road, their repayment is not necessarily a great burden on future generations, and the Minister would have a strong preference for sanctioning loans of this kind, rather than for projects which have a greater social than economic value, or whose economic benefit cannot be calculated except in terms of the distant future. Nevertheless, social projects are not necessarily excluded, and a recent Annual Report from Eastern Nigeria mentions loans raised for health centres, river craft, water supplies and 'Bailey bridges' as well as for projects whose economic advantages were more immediate.

A short chapter of a short book cannot deal properly with such a vast subject as local government finance, but the foregoing is a bare sketch of the more important aspects of the subject, so far as revenue is concerned.

CHAPTER 10

Northern Nigeria

So far we have been able to make some rough generalizations about local government in Eastern and Western Nigeria and Ghana. The situation in Northern Nigeria is so profoundly different that it requires a separate chapter.[1]

First we must clear away a misconception about 'the North'. It is very usual to hear people speak of local government in the Northern Region in terms of 'powerful Emirates', but it is not possible to generalize even about this one Region itself, and two things need to be borne in mind. First, that although there are indeed strong and well-organized emirates they are not themselves the units of local government; these are the 'Native Authorities', a term which the Northern Government has preferred to retain instead of the more popular expression 'local authorities'; it is true that the emirates are conterminous with native authorities, that is to say no emirate is split up into more than one native authority, but the two expressions are not strictly speaking interchangeable; while in areas which are not wholly Muslim a number of 'chieftaincies' have joined with others to form 'federated native authorities'. Second, that over substantial parts of the Region there are no emirates, since the Hausa-Fulani influence did not fully establish itself over such people as the Tiv, Nupe, Igala, Idoma or the Yorubas of Kabba, still less among the many so-called 'pagan' people of the Plateau. It is true that British administration tried to impose a tidy system of administration throughout the Region, and to introduce the successful pattern of emirate rule universally,

[1] I am indebted to Mr M. J. Campbell, of the Institute of Administration, Zaria, for reading this chapter and suggesting improvements.

but experience and growing knowledge of the people led them to modify this policy, and local government in such areas has long been 'conciliar', and sometimes fragmentary. There are in fact astonishing extremes in this country, from strong, disciplined and wealthy NAs in the emirates of the 'north of the North' to the rudimentary councils of primitive tribes in the hills and plateaux of the south-east.

This brings us to the first of two *fundamental* differences in the development of contemporary local government. Southern Nigeria and Ghana, faced with the task of modernizing and revitalizing their native authorities, introduced Ordinances which, though more flexible than the British legislation on which they were modelled, were expected to apply more or less uniformly throughout the respective countries; it is true that they were supposed to start experimentally in one or two places first and then to develop in the light of experience, but political pressures soon caused them to be applied wholesale instead of piecemeal, and within a short time of their enactment the terms of these Ordinances were being implemented everywhere. The Northern Government set its face against this, and while accepting the principle that the NAs must become more representative and more efficient, to keep pace with modern development, they resolved that this principle should be applied to each NA in the light of its history, its existing circumstances and its potentialities. To impose the same pattern of local government in Sokoto and on the Mambila Plateau would have been manifestly absurd. Accordingly, instead of providing for 'tiers' of councils with specific names, the Native Authority Law of 1954 made a much more flexible arrangement, under which the Premier could constitute as a native authority 'any chief or person, any chief or person in council or any chief or person *and* council', while the Minister of Local Government could similarly constitute 'any council or any group of persons'. The intention behind this was flexibility, which would start with the situation as it actually was, but would allow for change and progress; as we shall see in a moment, this intention has been fulfilled.

The second fundamental difference, though this applies more strongly in the emirates than elsewhere, is that native administration occupies, and has for long occupied, a place of importance in the administration of the country comparable to that of local government in Britain. This is not to suggest that the Council of an Emir bears the slightest outward resemblance to an English County Council, but that the degree of responsibility which it bears is comparable. While the Southern Nigerian and Ghanaian councils are gradually working up to a larger share in the administration of the country, though leaning heavily on government departmental assistance, the NAs virtually *are* the administration of the country. The larger ones carry responsibility for the major social services, and Kano, the largest, spends over £2 million a year and employs a salaried staff of over 5,000, as well as some 10,000 daily paid employees. An astonishing range of services is operated by the native authorities both on their own behalf and on behalf of the Government. It has often been said that whereas if the central government collapsed the NAs could carry on the administration of the country, if the NAs collapsed there would be complete disaster!

The reason for the strength of the native authorities, as is well known, is to be found in history. These kingdoms of the north of Nigeria, from which the present NAs are descended, were disciplined administrative units with—a vital point—an efficient system of taxation, long before the days of British rule, and Lord Lugard and his successors were therefore building what we now call local government on a more solid administrative and financial basis than elsewhere. We will try to illustrate the point factually a little later on.

Having mentioned two fundamental differences, which need constantly to be borne in mind, we pass to a description of the composition of the native authorities, their staff and their work. Other important differences will emerge, but they arise out of the practical application of local government, and are not fundamental in the same sense.

The law governing the subject is the Native Authority Law of 1954, which is more of a consolidating measure, and less of a radically new departure, than the local government laws of 1951–3 in Southern Nigeria and Ghana.

At the time of writing there are 70 native authorities. This figure in itself tells us something about the position of local government in Northern Nigeria, for these 70 authorities serve 25 million people,[1] whereas 12 million in the East are served by 107 authorities, and 10 million in the West by about the same number. This bears out the fact that the Northern authorities are fewer, larger and therefore more viable. In composition each of these NAs differs slightly from any other, but until very recently they could be classified into six main categories. First, there were those which consisted of a Chief and traditional members; second, a Chief, traditional members and nominated members; councils in these two categories would obviously have a strong authoritarian flavour. Then came three types of council with an elected element; the third category consisted of a Chief, traditional and nominated members and an elected *minority*; the fourth an elected element of 50 per cent; and the fifth an elected *majority*; sixthly, there was one council which was wholly elected. Since January 1, 1963, however, the Northern Government has resolved that all NA councils *must* include an elected element, and the present position, and also the recent trends, can be seen from the following tables:

	1958	1963
Chief and traditional members	2	0
Chief, traditional and nominated members	23	0
Chief, traditional and nominated members with elected minority	12	30
Chief, traditional and nominated members with 50 per cent elected	3	1
Chief, traditional and nominated members with elected majority	23	36
Wholly elected	1	1
'Caretaker' administration (temporary)	0	2
	64	70

[1] These figures are somewhat arbitrary, being based on the 1952 census figures plus 50 per cent.

The increase in the number of native authorities is accounted for by the accession of the Sardauna Province (formerly the Northern Cameroons).

Total number of elected councillors	535	854
Total number of *ex-officio* councillors	365	399
Total number of nominated councillors	367	427
	1,267	1,680

These figures illustrate the point that was made on the previous page, that the flexibility of the law has led to change, and from the representative point of view to progress. The figures may also help to dispel another misconception about the North, namely that it is more 'feudal' and less 'democratic' than other parts of West Africa. This of course begs the question of what is meant by 'democratic', but if we interpret the word to mean simply government by elected representatives the position is that in Southern Nigeria and Ghana (allowing for reserved seats for traditional members) every member was elected from the moment the new laws were implemented; whereas in the North the representative base has been broaded gradually until, within nine years of the Act of 1954, and within eleven years of the first NA councillors being elected under previous legislation in 1952 more than half the councils have an elected majority. Little is gained by arguing whether one method is 'better' or 'worse' than the other, since the meaning of such words is always relative; the real point of interest will be to see which system, in the course of time, gives greater satisfaction to the people as a whole.

There are two important minorities in the North for whom there is special representation on the native authorities. In some areas the nomadic Fulani, following their cattle over vast distances, are a significant part of the population, but they ignore and boycott elections, which have little or no meaning for them; they are accordingly represented by nominated members, appointed on the advice of the Fulani clans. Secondly, and this is more open to question, there are in certain parts, particularly in the urban and trading centres, large minorities from the other Regions of the country, especially of Ibos and Yorubas. In a more homogeneous country than Nigeria it would be supposed that people who had lived in the area of a local authority for a minimum period would be entitled to vote in their own right for members of local councils, but we are concerned with the facts as they are, and in practice representatives of these 'stranger' communities are nominated to the councils of those NAs where a substantial number of them live.

We now come to some important departures from what was written in previous chapters about the work of the councillors and the position of the staff. In Southern Nigeria and Ghana the intention was to emulate the British practice whereby councillors take no part in administration, and when, as often happened, they started giving directions to the staff or taking part in the ordinary work of the office, it was regarded as wrongful interference. In Northern Nigeria, however, councillors have long been associated with administration, partly because this was inherent in the traditional system handed down from long ago, and partly because in many areas of the North there were too few educated men in the 1950's to form local bureaucracies, or at any rate to provide the kind of senior local government officials who could take the initiative, make decisions and implement policy. Accordingly, NA councils bore some resemblance to miniature 'cabinets', in which selected councillors held portfolios and were put in charge of the various departments of the NA's work in return for a full-time salary. There would be a Member in charge of public health, education, works, agriculture, forestry and so on, and his responsibility, in the limited sphere of the NA, would be comparable to that of a Minister in the wider sphere of the Region. With the rapid increase of education, and more particularly of local government training, the quality of the staff of the NAs is showing consistent improvement, and as this happens the amount of detailed work done by the 'executive councillors' is diminishing. Nevertheless the principle is still followed that certain councillors are responsible for certain branches of work, and this is a radical difference from the system we have been discussing hitherto, where responsibility is vested in committees. There can be little doubt that as the committee system develops in the North, and especially in the emirates, the authority of the executive councillor will diminish further in proportion; already, by Ministerial direction, there are at least two committees set up by every NA, a finance committee and an establishment (or appointments) and staff committee.

Meanwhile, because of the great size of some of the NAS (the Bornu NA is larger than the Eastern Region of Nigeria) a standing Executive Committee is frequently appointed, instead of the various 'functional' committees of British practice. Indeed, the words 'cabinet' and 'parliamentary' have sometimes been used to distinguish between the very large NAs of the north of the Region and the smaller ones of the south and east, where an orthodox committee system is more practicable. Though neither adjective is very accurate they draw attention to a real difference, but one that is likely to diminish rather than grow.

The Native Authority Law includes another radical departure from the local government laws of Southern Nigeria and Ghana, in that it provides for the establishment of *subordinate* authorities, though this is perhaps not so much a departure as the continuance of a practice which used to be common to all these countries before 1950, but which has been discontinued elsewhere. British legislation on local government does not envisage the idea of subordinate authorities; some local authorities are large and some are small, but none is subordinate to another, each being independent of any authority except the central government in matters within its competence. Since Southern Nigeria and Ghana followed British legislation they adopted the system of 'tiers', which we have discussed earlier in the book.

These subordinate authorities in the North take a number

of different forms. In the first place the Law (sections 20–24) allows the Governor to establish subordinate native authorities in the full sense, and where this is done the subordinate authority must 'obey the orders of the native authority to which the Governor has directed that it shall be subordinate', but it may also exercise powers delegated to it by the superior authority. There are at present forty-nine subordinate native authorities in the Region. The Law does not in fact differentiate in any way between an NA and a subordinate NA and unless the superior authority restricts the powers or its subordinate by a published Order, the subordinate NA has the full powers of a native authority within the area of its jurisdiction. They are constituted in exactly the same way as native authorities, and they are most commonly found in the 'Federations', where the individual member authorities are subordinate to the Federation Council.

But the Law also allows (sections 54–5) the creation of administrative sub-areas within any native authority, and from the point of view of comparing Southern Nigeria, Ghana and Northern Nigeria these are of greater interest. Section 54 of the Law says that a native authority may 'divide the area under its jurisdiction . . . into districts, village areas, wards and such other administrative sub-areas as it may consider expedient', and goes on to say, in effect, that it may appoint district, village and ward heads. These heads constitute the most important difference between the North and elsewhere, so far as day-to-day administration is concerned. In the local authorities of the South there is no staff outside the headquarters office, except in so far as members of staff travel to different parts of their area in the course of their ordinary duties. The Northern NAs naturally have a similar, indeed much larger, staff at their headquarters, and as elsewhere its senior members are protected, both in their appointment and dismissal, by a higher authority, in this case the Premier; this protection is given to the secretary, treasurer, chief clerk, supervisor of works and to other officers whose salary is above a prescribed figure, at present £450 p.a.; it is also given to the chief of police, for whom there is no corresponding officer in local government in the South. But in addition there is this hierarchy of what might be called 'local government officials' right down to the smallest village or quarter of a town. The word 'official' is really not an appropriate one, since many of the posts of district and village heads are hereditary, or restricted to certain families, and they are often given the general description of 'traditional heads'; they are in fact persons of considerable status in their own right, and could hardly be described as employees. They are appointed by the emir or chief, subject to the approval of the Premier, and they represent something that does not exist in Southern Nigeria, that is a chain of authority reaching down directly from the NA to the smallest community within its borders. It is because of them that the mechanics of a large operation, like a census, an election or the annual tax collection, work more smoothly in this Region than elsewhere; indeed the equivalent of an annual census is taken for the assessment of tax, which is one of the major responsibilities of the district head, and a very high proportion of the tax—estimated at well over 90 per cent—is collected each year without difficulty.

It is sometimes thought that this chain of command, as we have called it, is in itself undemocratic, especially as the offices of heads are traditional, and derive from an ancient and authoritarian system. Again we are confronted with two points of view; twentieth-century bureaucratic procedures demand that every holder of a public office should appear on a short list and be interviewed by a committee; in the Northern Region a traditional office is being adapted to an increasingly representative form of local government; and there is no question that the *work* of a district head is thoroughly modern.

Be this as it may, the system is one of the most important departures from what was described in the earlier chapters of this book; it applies particularly to the emirates, since district heads do not exist, or exist in a modified form, in the conciliar native authorities of the south and east of the

Region; for example, in the Tiv NA their place is taken by 'clan heads', though even here district heads are just being introduced to cover groups of clans. Village headmen, on the other hand, are universal throughout the Region, and are the foundation on which native administration is built.

The same part of the Law (section 55) allows a native authority to establish by instrument a *council* for any administrative sub-area (or compels them to do so if the Minister of Local Government so directs), and it is interesting that the Instruments of all such councils prescribe that they shall contain an elected majority. There is, therefore, a greater degree of representative democracy at the 'grass-roots' than at the level of the NAs themselves, though as we have seen the NAs are always changing, and over half of them have now elected majorities. The village and ward councils have very little money of their own and consequently very little responsibility, but since 1954 the district councils have been acquiring an increasing amount. Usually they are permitted by the NA to keep for their own purposes a small proportion of the tax collected within their area, for example something of the order of 1s or 2s 6d per taxpayer in the rural areas, and on the basis of this they can frame their own estimates for minor local purposes. In some of the more urban areas, on the other hand, they have gone beyond this elementary stage, and their budgets are equivalent to the average budgets of local authorities in Southern Nigeria and Ghana; for example, the Waje Council of Kano, which is a subordinate council, now handles a budget of more than £60,000. In the rural areas the district and village councils are providing an excellent training ground for democracy among the less sophisticated peoples.

Although it is the purpose of this chapter to draw attention to the differences between the North and the South, it is not suggested that either has necessarily anything to learn from the other. The traditional heads of the North are both possible and necessary for reasons which do not apply in the South; possible, because they derive from long-established custom; necessary, because the native authority areas are so very much larger. There is a blend of tradition and modernity in the local government system of the North, and it is interesting that control at the highest level is divided between the Premier and the Minister of Local Government, the Premier retaining personal responsibility for some of the affairs of the councils in the emirates, and the reserve powers governing the appointment and dismissal of NA staff. This stems partly from the fact that when the Native Authority Law was enacted in 1954 the Premier undertook the portfolio of Local Government, and has retained some of the powers which then attached to him. This, however, is not the whole explanation, since there was a similar combination of portfolios in the other Regions in the early days of local government. The retention of the Premier's direct powers in the North probably symbolizes the much closer personal contact which exists between the Premier and the Cabinet on the one hand and the native authorities on the other; Members of Parliament, including members of the Cabinet, are themselves members of their local NA councils in their own right, a practice which is otherwise only found in Sierra Leone, where members of the Legislature are *ex officio* members of their local 'district' council (see p. 154).

There is one other kind of subordinate council, but we need only mention it in passing, partly because it has only advisory powers and partly because it is in any case in decline. This is the so-called 'outer council', which a native authority may also establish by instrument, a 'representative and consultative body' whose purpose is to 'render assistance and advice'; it has no executive powers or duties and is becoming increasingly redundant as the NAs themselves become more representative. Its original purpose was to bridge the gap between the NA and the people in the days when the former was hardly representative at all. Its usefulness is also being diminished by the new provincial councils which will be mentioned later in this chapter.

We turn now to the functions of the native authorities, as shown in their expenditure, and to the sources of their revenue. A good deal of what was said in Chapters 6 and 9 is equally relevant to Northern Nigeria, and we shall not repeat it here, but shall confine ourselves to the significant differences between this Region and the others. On p. 17 we mentioned that in a recent year (1961–2) local authorities in Eastern Nigeria spent a little over £4¼ million, and in the West nearly £8½ million. The corresponding figure for the North in the same year was nearly £10 million, plus another £2 million on commercial undertakings (which, however, showed a small net loss) and capital projects. Broadly speaking there were no great differences in the ways in which it was spent, since education (nearly £2 million) was again the largest single item, recurrent works the second largest (£1,371,000) and public health services (£993,000) the *fourth*; again, relatively small amounts were spent on agriculture, forestry and veterinary services, and there is evidence, as in the South, that the native authorities do not take such a keen interest in them as do the corresponding departments of the central government. Nevertheless, the proportion of total expenditure which went to agricultural and veterinary services was strikingly higher than in the East or West (2 per cent on agriculture compared with 0·4 per cent and 0·1 per cent, and 1·5 per cent on veterinary services compared with 0·2 per cent and virtually nil). The cost of administration (about 13 per cent) was almost identical in spite of the closer administration of the North, an example of the economy of larger scale authorities.

The most important difference was in the proportion spent on law and order, judging this by the cost of police and prisons, and leaving out the native courts, which more than paid for themselves.[1] The proportionate cost was more than twice that in Western Nigeria, and totalled £1,300,000. This bears out the fact that the maintenance of law and order is primarily a responsibility of the native authorities and not, as in the South, of the Nigerian Federal Police; indeed, the NA police normally deal with over 75 per cent of 'the crime

[1] In Eastern and Western Nigeria, on the other hand, the local courts represented a net financial loss.

of this Region. The Nigerian police have very small establishments in the North, and those principally in the capital and in the commercial and railway towns. As a function of local government, maintaining law and order is in a category by itself, and cannot reasonably be compared in importance with education, works or public health, but even in actual cost it comes third, after education and works, but above public health. It is appropriate that the part of the law which describes the powers and duties of native authorities should lay more stress, and go into more detail, on the prevention of crime than the other laws.

Another very considerable section of this part of the law deals with the establishment, management and closing of markets, in much greater detail than the corresponding laws elsewhere.

The Law follows the pattern of the Western Law, however, in setting out the functions of native authorities more in terms of their legislative powers than in terms of 'powers and duties'; that is to say of their power to make by-laws, or, to use the word actually employed, 'rules'. These rules cover very much the same ground as was described on page 78, the most striking addition being the power to regulate the use of land. The Southern Nigerian laws also make some elaborate provisions about land, and the Ghanaian Act some shorter and simpler ones, but these deal principally with the power of local authorities to acquire and dispose of land for their corporate purposes. The Northern Nigerian Law gives NAs the power to make rules controlling the *use* of land within their areas of jurisdiction, and these apply particularly to the control of customary rights of occupancy and the proper farming of land, including anti-erosion measures, the control of stock and the maintenance of fences, drains, wind-breaks, etc.; though some of these powers have since been modified by the Land Tenure Law of 1962, which, for example, vests the alienation of land to 'strangers', formerly a power of the NAs, in the Minister of Land and Survey, though there is still power in the Law for him to delegate this to NAs if he thinks fit.

These 'rules', like the by-laws in other Regions, require the approval of the Governor before they are effective, in order that there shall be no conflict either with other rules or with the policy of the Government. We said a moment ago that they covered much the same ground as was described on p. 78, but there is in fact one slight difference that is worth mentioning. In certain matters, under section 43 of the Law, native authorities may enact subsidiary legislation which does *not* require any covering approval. They may do this by making 'orders', as distinct from 'rules', and the matters in which they may do so can broadly be described as 'nuisances'. For example, they may on their own authority prohibit or restrict gambling, the possession of weapons, the burning off of grass or bush or interference with paths or roads; they also have considerable powers of 'prohibiting, restricting, controlling or regulating' all kinds of noise, including motor-car horns, radio sets and loud-speakers. They may also require 'any native to cultivate land to such an extent and with such crops as will secure an adequate supply of food for the support of such native and of those dependent on him'.

With these two or three exceptions the powers and duties of NAs are very similar to those in the South and in Ghana. What distinguishes them is not so much what they do as the scale upon which they do it. To put it in a nutshell, a considerably smaller number of local authorities are spending a considerably larger sum of money, which means that each is spending more, and can therefore operate more efficiently and economically. As we have already said, there is no uniformity about this, and it is only in the larger emirates that NAs are comparable in scope with British authorities; nevertheless the general level of revenue and expenditure is higher than elsewhere, as we can see from looking at a few examples taken from the top, the middle and the bottom ranges.

At the top we observe, in descending order, Kano (estimated ordinary revenue in 1961–2: £2,098,110), Bornu (£999,140), Sokoto (£943,354), Katsina (£887,504) and Zaria

(£508,513). Local authorities which spend between half a million and 2 million pounds in a year can obviously shoulder work which has to be done by the central government elsewhere, and these NAs have in the past built and maintained hospitals, main roads, waterworks and electricity undertakings before these were undertaken by the Regional or Federal Government. The thing which has given them their 'take-off', to use a fashionable expression, is that their resources have allowed them to employ skilled engineering staff, including expatriates when necessary, and to maintain adequate yards, workshops, fleets of vehicles and engineering equipment. In the middle ranges there are NAs which vary from Tiv (£471,273) and Ilorin (£351,550) to a considerable group like Biu (£93,699) and Bauchi (£82,314). At the bottom there are, for example, Kazaure (the smallest emirate) (£64,480), Bedde (£48,571) and Ningi (£41,602). In other words the smallest in the North is roughly equivalent to the average in the South (excluding, of course, the big southern towns).

It must be emphasized that this favourable comparison with the South arises from size, population and—as a consequence—financial resources. The problems which beset local government everywhere in West Africa—lack of drive, ability and integrity—are as common in Northern Nigeria as anywhere else. Our argument is simply that greater financial viability and closer supervision enable them to be more effective.

To round off this comparison, a few words must be said about the NAs sources of revenue.

An accurate comparison would in fact be very difficult to make, since the allocation of tax revenue between central and local government is on a different basis. In Ghana and Southern Nigeria both central and local authorities may tax the general population, and the frontiers between them have not yet reached final definition. In Northern Nigeria, since the passing of the Personal Tax Law of 1962, $87\frac{1}{2}$ per cent of the general tax, now known as the 'community tax', is retained by the native authorities; the Regional Government derives its own tax revenue from central 'income tax', which is clearly distinguished from the community tax in the 1962 Law.[1] Moreover, the amount of the community tax raised locally by the NAs is relatively greater than in the South because of more efficient assessment and collection, and it is supplemented by the tax known as 'jangali'—a tax upon cattle—to the extent, in 1961-2, of £1,168,822. The assessment of the community tax, though ultimately a responsibility of the Provincial Commissioner, is in practice made by traditional methods by the district and village heads, and is a graduated tax based upon ability to pay.

The result of this is that the native authorities derive the great bulk of their revenue from locally assessed and collected tax, and only to a small extent from Government grants. To be precise, community tax and jangali amounted to no less than £8,142,648 out of a total revenue of £11,976-753, while only £1,439,473 came from Government grants. This is in striking contrast to the figures quoted on p. 108, which showed that grants reached 52 per cent in Eastern Nigeria and 40 per cent in Western Nigeria and Ghana. This illustrates the general point that native administration in Northern Nigeria occupies a more important and less dependent place in the general administration of the country. The balance of the revenue comes from sources very similar to the other countries, e.g. fees, licences and a number of miscellaneous receipts.

Of the relatively small Government grant of £1·4 million the largest amount goes towards aiding education (£748,000) and a much larger proportion than elsewhere (£300,000) to subsidizing the NA police.

Before leaving the comparison altogether, it is worth repeating that the relatively favourable position of local government in the North is a result not of recent politics but of a long tradition of administration dating from pre-British days. The native authorities of today are reaping

---

[1] The Commissioner of Revenue may, however, appoint an NA as the tax collecting agency, in which case it retains 20 per cent for its services as a collector.

the crops sown in the nineteenth century and nurtured during the first half of the twentieth.

The large towns of the Northern Region do not present a problem of such physical magnitude as elsewhere. For example, in Western Nigeria there are six towns with populations of over 100,000 (including Ibadan which is approaching three-quarters of a million), all of them unplanned, seriously congested and lacking in sanitary and other basic services. In the North, Kano (estimated population 195,000) is the only town above 100,000, and all the Northern towns have more space, thus making planned development in the future a good deal easier. They have, however, a considerable administrative problem to solve, as the larger ones have been allowed to grow up in a very haphazard manner. In Kano itself, for example, the Old City is an integral part of the Kano NA; but communities outside the city walls, including the 'sabon gari' with its large immigrant population, are the responsibility of the Kano Waje town council, a subordinate council of the NA; while the so-called 'township', the modern commercial, industrial and government area, is directly administered by the central government. Thus, what ought to be considered as one large urban complex, with common needs and complementary functions, is wastefully administered as three separate towns. However, both the physical and administrative replanning of Kano is under active investigation, and the Kano Greater Planning Authority, set up under the Town and Country Planning Law of October 1962, has taken over the planning and development of Kano City, Kano Waje and the township.

We shall conclude this chapter by picking up some of the threads of Chapter 8 (Local authorities and the Central Goverment), since this is a matter on which the experience of the North can throw some fresh light. We remarked that the trend in Ghana was for the central government, through the politically appointed regional and district commissioners and their staffs, to ensure that the local authorities were exercising their functions properly and keeping their finances in good order; and that in Eastern Nigeria provincial commissioners and secretaries were performing a somewhat similar task; in their case there is as yet no formal local government inspectorate, as in Ghana, but the provincial commissioner's office and staff are in themselves a kind of local authority, using the expression in its alternative sense of 'the local arm of the central government', and the provincial secretary has specific powers over the local authorities.

Similar developments are taking place in Northern Nigeria, though the background is different and the problem altogether more complicated. Unlike the South, it has never been supposed that provincial government, in one form or another, could be dispensed with; on the contrary the aim, though pursued rather fitfully and hesitantly, has been to increase its importance. This is understandable, partly because provincial administration under a resident has, like the NAs themselves, always been a pillar of government; and partly because the immense size of the Region, coupled in many areas with poor communications, would have made a centralized government, such as could in theory have been carried on from Enugu or Ibadan, or even from Accra, a physical impossibility. There was another reason, some six or seven years ago, for supposing that the time was ripe for enhancing the status of provincial administration, a reason which lay in the native authorities themselves. We have so far remarked only upon their undoubted effectiveness, but this is not by any means the whole story, since there were certain aspects of the NAs which gave cause for dissatisfaction. One was that some of them interpreted the political independence of the Region to mean that they themselves would be more independent, and they began to think of themselves almost in the manner of small sovereign states, to an extent which no Government could tolerate in its local authorities, and which might even have endangered the political unity of the Region. Another was that they are grossly uneven in size, as we have seen from a brief glance at their revenues; every province contains more than one

NA and most contain a considerable number.[1] Possibly Katsina represents the most logical form of administration, since the province (the political unit), the emirate (the traditional unit) and the native authority (the local government unit), are almost identical, the only exception being the small Emirate of Daura which is included in the provincial boundary. But elsewhere, as in Sokoto or Bornu, a typical pattern is that within the province there is one outstandingly large and important NA and several small ones, the total area and population of which are insignificant in relation to the principal one; this unevenness is also apparent in the southern provinces of the Region, which can mean that the services provided in different parts of a province are also uneven. Finally, not all the NAs, and particularly not the smaller ones, showed equal interest or ability in providing some of the less popular but vitally important services such as agricultural extension, veterinary and forestry work, soil conservation and pest control; neither were they at all comparable in their ability to provide major constructional works such as main roads and schools.

In the mind of the Regional Government, therefore, two trends happened to coincide in the mid-1950's. The central ministries were feeling the need to decentralize their departmental work, and to place their major undertakings on a systematic provincial basis; and at the same time they felt the need to put certain NA services on a more centralized, i.e. provincial, footing. This clearly pointed to an outright form of provincial government, and the possibilities of this kind of government were outlined in the Report of a Special Commissioner in 1957.[2] There is no space to discuss this Report, but it pointed in the direction not only of stronger provincial government, but of provincial administrators, who would be virtually indistinguishable from French

[1] There are thirteen provinces, including the new Sardauna Province, formerly the Northern Cameroons.
[2] Provincial Authorities: Report by Mr R. S. Hudson, CMG, Govt. Printer, Kaduna.

Prefects, and who would be supported by provincial executives and elected provincial assemblies.

These suggestions were not adopted, and matters hung fire for some years. Recently, however, they have gained a new interest with the passing of the Provincial Administration Law of 1962. This Law rejects the most essential proposals of the Special Commissioner, but it does establish a new kind of provincial administration; each province becomes the responsibility of a Minister, holding the office of 'provincial commissioner', and a 'provincial secretary' assists him in the relationship of a permanent secretary. This Law specifically empowers the Premier, through the provincial commissioner, to give directions to native authorities in the performance of their duties. Consultative provincial councils have now also been constituted, though these only meet twice a year, and are, so to speak, informal provincial parliaments. These developments do not specifically detract from the powers of the native authorities; on the other hand a new type of 'local government' has been established, in the alternative meaning of that expression, and one moreover which has definite powers of direction over the native authorities. Thus, as in Eastern Nigeria, we see two widely different concepts of local government existing side by side and the former independence of the native authorities would appear to have been diminished.

To sum up, both past history and contemporary developments are distinctive in Northern Nigeria, and what is happening there needs to be put into the general pool of ideas about local government in West Africa, into which we shall dip in the concluding chapter.

CHAPTER 11

Sierra Leone

SIERRA LEONE also needs a separate chapter. In common with Northern Nigeria, its present local government stems not from radical legislation in the early 1950's, but from an older, and in this case a 'tribal' system, the main features of which survive into the present structure; and in common with Northern and Eastern Nigeria its principal administrative divisions (provinces) have been brought into the political structure of the Government by the appointment of 'Resident Ministers' of Cabinet rank. Apart from these two similarities the system is, for English-speaking West Africa, unique.

The City of Freetown is the oldest municipality in West Africa, and the Freetown peninsula, which used to be called the 'colony' but which is now known as the 'rural areas' of Freetown, has its own distinguishing features. But apart from these, and over the whole of what used to be called the 'protectorate' of Sierra Leone, there is a uniform pattern of local administration which comprises:

146 'chiefdoms'
12 'districts'
3 'provinces'

Within this pattern are three 'townships'.

It will be convenient to adopt a slightly different approach in describing how this system works, by treating each of these units in turn.

THE CHIEFDOMS

The paramount chiefs are the traditional agents of local

administration, and the chiefdoms are still the base of the local government pyramid, and are fundamental to the government of the country, though the prestige of the chiefs suffered a considerable blow in the years 1954 and 1955. This arose partly from the fact that with the stirrings of nationalism in the early 1950's, but without any legislative changes in the system of local government, the powers of the expatriate district commissioners were considerably reduced, and their role altered from the executive to the advisory. This was somewhat premature, for a number of chiefs, removed from the firm control of the DC, started to behave badly and to use their powers for personal extortion. There were widespread riots against them, resulting in a Commission of Enquiry from whose Report they emerged with little credit.[1] In the years since then, however, they have done much to recover their position.

Chiefdoms are established under an Ordinance of 1938 known as the Tribal Authorities Ordinance, and the correct name for what elsewhere would be known as the council is in fact the 'tribal authority', though they are customarily referred to as 'native administrations'; the tribal authority, in the words of the Ordinance, means 'the paramount chief, the chiefs, the councillors and men of note elected by the people according to native law and custom, approved by the Governor', and generally numbers between forty and sixty members. Local government in Sierra Leone is therefore based on traditional bodies and not, as in Ghana and Southern Nigeria, on councils predominantly elected by secret ballot.

As organs of local government the tribal authorities have been neither representative nor efficient; their meetings have been infrequent, often no more than twice a year, their government autocratic and in the hands of ruling cliques, and the powers of the chiefs arbitrary. These facts have been recognized by the Government since 1954 by their encourage-

[1] Report of a Commission of Enquiry into Disturbances in the Provinces, November 1955 to March 1956 (published by the Crown Agents on behalf of the Government of Sierra Leone).

ment—administratively and not by legislation—of 'chiefdom councils' and 'chiefdom committees'. The former were intended to make the tribal authorities more representative, by compelling them to take into consultation both the chiefdom members on the district council (see below, p. 154) and a number of members (specifically to include young men) who would be elected by taxpayers from the different sections of the chiefdom. The chiefdom committees were intended to make them more efficient by appointing the more literate and able members of the tribal authority, together with others, to form a kind of standing Finance and General Purposes Committee which would keep the business affairs of the authority under constant review. Neither councils nor committees have operated with any system or uniformity throughout the country, but they have to some extent modernized the tribal authorities and brought them closer to the realities of twentieth-century administration.

The position of the chief himself is not easy to define, and has more in common with that of chiefs in Uganda and other parts of East and Central Africa than of the paramount chiefs of Ghana or the obas of Western Nigeria. On the one hand, he is chosen by traditional methods and his office carries, on proper occasions, the ceremony and dignity associated with traditional chieftainship; on the other hand for most of his working life he more resembles a hard-working local government officer or civil servant, as he is the principal executive officer of the tribal authority, working each day in authority's office, and the effectiveness of the authority depends to a great extent on his ability. He is in fact in the rather invidious position, like 'executive' chiefs in many other parts of Africa, of being part natural local ruler, part local government official and part civil servant.[1] However, there is no doubt about his importance in the general scheme of government; it is said that in the early days of the nationalists' demand for self-government Dr Nkrumah in

[1] The word 'chief' as used in English-speaking Africa is one of the most unsatisfactory words in the English language, as it has been used to describe, in a legal sense, everything from a king, as in Ashanti or Buganda, to a minor civil servant wearing a uniform, as in Kenya.

Ghana appealed to the people for support but in Sierra Leone Sir Milton Margai appealed to the chiefs.

As local government units the chiefdoms are small, and their work considerably more restricted than that of local councils in other parts of West Africa. On a very rough average they cover the area occupied by about 3,000 adult male taxpayers, a good deal more in the industrial areas where iron ore and diamonds are mined (e.g. close on 6,000 in Port Loko District), and a good deal less in the poorer and more rural areas (e.g. about 1,800 in Pujehun District). Their principal activity is still the native court,[1] which in the other coastal territories has been gradually separated from the work of the local councils. The paramount chief, however, is not the court president, who is now elected by the tribal authority; the separation of the chief from the court was made to remove doubts about the impartiality of the president, and to this extent a beginning has been made with distinguishing between executive and judicial functions. These courts are, as elsewhere, largely occupied with such matters as dowry, debt, inheritance, land, etc., and in certifying cases of theft or violence to the magistrate's court. In other words the chief activity of the tribal authorities lies in discharging their responsibility for 'order and good government' and the 'prevention of crime'.

This, however, is by no means the end of their potential responsibilities. Their powers and duties under the Ordinance are not dissimilar from those of local authorities elsewhere, but because of their restricted means they are carried out in a more modest fashion. They may 'issue orders' on such matters as water pollution, burning-off, cultivation, the movement of livestock and may control nuisances. They may also make by-laws, subject to the usual approvals, on the normal range of activities of small local authorities such as markets, slaughter houses, wash places, the sale of food and drink, street trading, fees, licences and building lines. An

---

[1] By an Act of 1963 the native courts have been re-named 'local courts', their area of jurisdiction, both in civil and criminal cases, has been extended, and they have been brought into the normal appelate system of the country.

interesting point is that orders and by-laws must be 'orally promulgated', i.e. publicly announced, as well as being 'posted in the court barri or market place of the principal town of the chiefdom'.

Another point of interest is that one type of order which a tribal authority may make concerns the registration of births and deaths. This is not of course unusual, for there are similar provisions in other West African local government laws (see p. 73); what *is* unusual is that registration works satisfactorily in chiefdoms throughout the country. Elsewhere it is considered an extremely difficult thing to achieve, and usually only works with any degree of efficiency in selected urban areas; but in Sierra Leone there appears to be no difficulty in enforcing it throughout the country in these small local authorities which are in many ways 'backward' compared with those of Nigeria and Ghana.

Otherwise their powers to issue orders and to make by-laws have not been very extensively or imaginatively used.

The chiefdoms also make small contributions to education, medical and health services, agriculture, forestry and roads, though the main responsibility for these falls on the higher 'District Councils' or on the provincial departments of the central government. In the case of roads the contribution may take the form of communal labour to maintain minor roads rather than of financial expenditure.

Finally, the chiefdom is the tax assessment and tax collecting authority, a point which will be discussed a little later in dealing with their revenue.

The chiefdoms are strictly controlled by higher authority, and have never been given the freedom which was at one time given to the local authorities in Eastern Nigeria, or is at present given to the 'financially autonomous' councils of Western Nigeria. A higher authority must approve most of the things they do, including their budgeting, and may compel them to do things which they are failing to do. The 'higher authority' was in colonial days the (Provincial) Chief Commissioner and the Governor, but their powers have now become vested in the Provincial Resident Minister.

The tribal authorities of Sierra Leone budget for sums varying from £5,000 to £15,000. The scale of their activity may be understood from the following expenditure budget in a recent year of a tribal authority well above the average in size, i.e. about 6,000 taxpayers:

		£
1.	Precept to District Council	3,000
2.	Hereditary officials	2,721
3.	Administration	1,002
4.	Native Court	1,559
5.	Messengers	1,772
6.	Prison	189
7.	Education	364
8.	Medical and Health	876
9.	Agriculture	132
10.	Forestry	590
11.	Works	496
12.	Miscellaneous	1,091
		£13,792

The first and largest item is of particular interest. The finances of the district councils, which we shall be discussing in a moment, rest largely on the 'precept' from the constituent chiefdoms. The device of the precept was, as we have seen (p. 82), introduced into the local government legislation of Ghana and Southern Nigeria in the early 1950's, but never worked satisfactorily and has been abandoned in Eastern Nigeria and Ghana. In Sierra Leone, on the other hand, it works reasonably well. Human nature being what it is, there is the usual grumbling in the chiefdoms at having to pass so much money over to the district councils, and complaints that they waste it; in practice it is paid without undue difficulty, and it is not altogether uncommon for the services of the district council to be regarded as good value for money. The £3,000 represents 10s a head for 6,000 taxpayers, out of a total individual tax of 25s.

The £364 which is spend on education is for scholarships in the form of half school fees for chiefdom children in secondary schools. The small sum for agriculture is to pay a man in charge of a seedling nursery, the £590 on forestry for paying forest guards, and the £496 for works is for helping the district council with communal labour on unskilled road construction and maintenance; the money is actually spent on food and customary 'dashes', an unconventional but at the same time sensible and economical way of getting public work done.

The revenue of the same council was made up as follows:

	£
1. Local tax (6,000 at 25s)	7,500
2. Court receipts	3,100
3. Grants from the central government for administration	1,563
4. Miscellaneous	74
5. Licences	295
6. Fees	20
7. Revenue-earning projects (e.g. markets)	1,094
	£13,646

With regard to item (3) it is the practice of the central government to pay direct to the chiefdoms 50 per cent of the remuneration of the Paramount Chief (who might earn something in the neighbourhood of £1,200 a year), the clerks and the messengers.

Since the chiefdoms are the tax assessment and collecting authorities, it will be appropriate to say something at this point about local taxation (the word 'rate' is not used except in connection with the property rate, which is being introduced into the townships). This is controlled by the Local Tax Ordinance of 1955, which prescribes that every male over twenty-one shall be liable to pay tax (as compared with sixteen in Ghana and eighteen in Nigeria). Tax assessment committees are appointed by the tribal authority to determine the amount of the tax each year. There is no graduated tax apart from the central government income tax, which does not apply to incomes under £300 a year, and which is only just beginning to be levied outside the main urban centres of population; in most of the chiefdoms £300 a year would be far above the level of income of the vast majority of people. The tax is normally payable to a chief or headman, who receives a commission of 1s 3d a taxpayer, but employers of labour may be appointed by the Minister to collect the tax from their employees. It is fairly standard practice throughout the country for the tax to be fixed at 25s–30s, and for the district council precept to be 10s.

It is this Ordinance which prescribes that district councils may issue precepts on the tribal authorities, subject to the approval of the Resident Minister, but it need not necessarily be the same precept for every tribal authority in the district council area.

DISTRICT COUNCILS

Although the name 'district council' is a familiar one, there is in fact nothing to correspond to the Sierra Leone district councils in the other West African countries. This is because they were not originally intended only—or even primarily—as organs of local government, though the possibility of this development was foreshadowed. They were in the first place simply groupings of chiefdoms through which the Government intended to channel a certain proportion of the funds voted for development under a Development Plan of 1949.[1] This in itself could have been a sound and encouraging basis on which to reform and modernize local government, since the weakness in Southern Nigeria and Ghana since the early 1950's has been that a somewhat elaborate structure of local government has been erected without very much inside it; that is to say, there has been a hierarchy of councils with extensive powers on paper, but with little opportunity to exercise those powers because of the lack of funds. To bring a new type of authority into being for the specific purpose of spending money on development—money which would be provided by the central government and the Produce Marketing Board—could have brought a greater sense of reality to local government than elsewhere.

This point of view is summed up in the Childs Report itself:[2]

[1] The Childs Report on Economic Development in Sierra Leone, 1949.
[2] Quoted in the Report of the Commission of Enquiry into Disturbances in the Provinces, op. cit.

'At the end of 1949 the Government decided to devolve much of its plan of economic development on to districts. The resources . . . would be pooled in district councils . . . This decision offered an opportunity not only for developing the internal economy . . . but also for an important step forward in the organization of local government . . . The criticism that local government bodies have sometimes been set up as an administrative exercise without any clear idea what they can do can certainly not be levelled at this measure. Councils were established because there was a practical job to be done and an organization required to do it.'

The venture was only partly successful. It is true that from 1951 to 1956, at first under the chairmanship of the district commissioner and from 1954 under a president appointed by the Governor in Council, the district councils fulfilled the role allotted to them, among other things spending grants of £5,000 a year on agricultural improvements as a contribution to the wider development plan. From the point of view of building a new kind of local authority, however, there was one serious weakness, namely that the district councils were not fulfilling the role of local authorities but were simply doing local agency work for the central government, spending, under direction, sums of money provided for specific purposes. This may have been useful, but it was not a proper training for local democracy, and the removal of the district commissioners as chairmen in 1954 did not add even to their usefulness, as the presidents who took their place interfered, in a manner all too familiar in Nigeria and Ghana, with the secretary and staff in the execution of their duties.

However, the intention to build them up into new multipurpose local authorities was followed, and was embodied in the District Councils (Amendment) Ordinance of 1954. This Ordinance, which was the one which removed the district commissioners from the chairmanships, also introduced the precept on the chiefdoms as a new source of revenue to supplement the Government grant, extended their range of functions, and slightly altered their membership. It is the Ordinance under which the councils at present operate, and we may now briefly describe their composition, their work and their finances.

Each district is divided into 'wards', based very roughly on 1,000 taxpayers; since chiefdoms vary from about 2,000 to 6,000 taxpayers, it follows that there will be several wards in each chiefdom. The district council then consists of the chief, one member elected from each ward, *the local members of the legislative council* (another interesting departure from the usual practice elsewhere) and a few co-opted members. A full district council may number some sixty to eighty members, which raises the question of what is a workable size for an effective council in local government. Certainly this is too large in the circumstances of West Africa, which is borne out by the fact that few district councils meet more often than the statutory minimum, which is twice a year; even this may cost £1,000 a year—a very large sum in relative terms—merely in paying for councillors' travelling expenses and sitting fees. It follows from this that the council itself is not an effective body for transacting business, but has more of the character of a local parliament, in which there is very little restriction on the subjects which may be discussed. In practice all kinds of subjects which appear to have no relation to the work of local government are raised and debated. Meetings of this kind have, of course, considerable value, and one particularly useful feature of them is that they provide technical officers of the Government, or indeed eminent visitors to the country, with an opportunity to address a representative audience on matters of importance.

The more serious and regular work of the council, however, is effectively done by the Finance and General Purposes Committee, and a few other committees, which meet monthly.

District councils are expected to provide their own secretary, treasurer, works supervisor and subordinate staff, but in most districts there are central or provincial government 'assigned' staff; that is to say education, health, agricultural and forestry officers who are assigned to work in the district.

An assigned officer is not, however, the same thing as a seconded officer, for he continues to be employed by the Government, which pays his salary.

When we come to consider the functions of district councils, we find another interesting variation from the British-type legislation adopted in Ghana and Southern Nigeria. Such legislation is, as we have seen, governed by the doctrine of *ultra vires*, which restricts local authorities to doing only those things which the law specifically entitles them to do. The functions of the district councils are cast in much more general terms; their purpose is:

(1) To promote the development of the District and the welfare of the people with the funds at its disposal.

(2) To advise on any matter brought before it by direction of the Minister.

(3) To make recommendations to the Government on matters affecting the welfare of the people as a whole.

This is in remarkable contrast to, for example, the existing Eastern Nigeria Law, with its list of ninety-one specific things that a county council may do.

In addition to these general functions the Resident Minister may empower a district council to purchase building material for disposal to any tribal authority or person; lend money to any tribal authority or person; and guarantee contracts. It may be said at once, however, and the matter disposed of, that some of these functions were exercised in past years, with disastrous results. Many loans have had to be written off as irrecoverable, and these powers are no longer being awarded.

On paper, therefore, the district councils are free to go ahead with development of any kind. In practice their work is extremely restricted, and consists almost entirely of building and maintaining roads and primary schools. It has to be remembered that in communications especially Sierra Leone is some years behind Ghana and Nigeria, and that for the forseeable future the energies of district councils and tribal authorities alike could be largely absorbed in the most fundamental of all development work, i.e. joining villages together by road and thus enabling farmers to get their produce out of the bush and into the market. Even so and in spite of the fact that these are the most important tasks of the district councils, only about half of them are able to employ a qualified works superintendent or to maintain a reasonably well equipped works yard. Apart from the construction of simple bridges and culverts, road building is still largely a matter of pick, shovel and 'elbow grease'. Lack of funds and lack of skilled employees keep the district councils' work within these modest limits.

In the two main activities of school and road building, Government grants are given at the rate of £43 and £38 per mile for the two recognized classes of district road; in the case of schools the Government gives 60 per cent of the original capital cost, but their maintenance is wholly a charge on the district councils.

The scale of expenditure of the twelve district councils is roughly comparable to that of a county council in Eastern Nigeria, a district council in Western Nigeria or a local council in Ghana. This is the level at which the most valid comparison can be made, since the Sierra Leone chiefdom would correspond to the lower tier authorities elsewhere. The estimated expenditure of a typical district council in a recent year totalled £59,000, of which schools and roads absorbed £36,000. The figure for schools was £20,000 (£12,500 capital and £7,500 maintenance), and for roads £16,000. Minor sums were spent on agriculture, forestry and public health.

In the estimated revenue of the same district council the major sources were:

	£
Grants for specific development projects	16,000
Ordinary grants in aid	14,000
Contributions from chiefdoms (precepts)	15,000

In other words grant aid from the Government accounted for two thirds of the estimated revenue, and the precept from the chiefdoms to a third.

THE TOWNSHIPS

Outside the capital city of Freetown there are very few towns of any considerable size, the largest being Bo, Kenema and Makeni, the three provincial capitals, and the rapidly growing iron ore town of Marampa-Lunsar. Bo has been a township for a considerable time, under a special Bo Town Council Ordinance, but the government of towns has now been regularized by the Townships Ordinance of 1959, and Kenema and Makeni are now governed by its provisions.

The Ordinance provides that the membership of a town council shall comprise a president, who shall be the paramount chief of the chiefdom in which the town is situated, two councillors elected from each ward, two members nominated by the Resident Minister and two members appointed by the local tribal authority. A chairman (as distinct from the president) is elected annually, all members hold office for four years, and qualifications include literacy in English. Councils are expected to appoint a town clerk, treasurer, medical officer of health, surveyor and bailiff, though their appointment and dismissal are subject to Ministerial approval. In practice, because of the shortage of qualified men, the minister of health and the surveyor are more likely to be provincial officers devoting part of their time to the affairs of the town council.

The powers and duties of the town councils follow the usual lines; their mandatory duties involve sanitation and the upkeep of roads, streets, culverts, markets, slaughter houses and cemeteries; their permissive powers include such things as planning and layouts, lighting, fire precautions and washing and bathing places; they may also impose licence fees on traders, hotels and lodging houses, money lenders, sellers of palm wine and patent medicines, and also on vehicles, other than motor vehicles. They have also the more controversial power, which does not appear in all types of local government law, of engaging 'with the approval of the Minister . . . in any form of public undertaking, trading or industry'.

The relationship of the town council to the authorities surrounding it is of some importance, since certain of the powers and duties just mentioned are exercised also by the chiefdom or the district council; when a town council is established it *takes over* these duties; that is to say, there is not a 'two-tier' system of government within the township area, except for those services which are directly provided by the Government.

Finally, the town councils have the power to levy rates on property, some details of which have already been given on page 118, but the payment of a property rate does not exempt a man from the local tax levied in the surrounding chiefdom.

FREETOWN

The Freetown City Council has a particular historical interest, since it was first established by a Royal Charter granted by King George III in 1799, and has enjoyed the prestige of a mayor and aldermen since that date. It was created a municipality in a more modern sense in 1893, and is thus one of the oldest municipalities in Africa.[1] The subsequent history of the municipal council, however, was neither happy nor distinguished, and was characterized by refusals to pay rates, by dishonesty and corruption, and by inefficiency. After vicissitudes lasting for more than fifty years it was re-established under its existing Act in 1948.

The present council consists of a mayor, three aldermen and nine elected councillors, one alderman and three councillors being elected in each of three wards. A further six councillors are appointed by the Governor-General, making a total of nineteen, a sensible and manageable number which is in contrast to the unnecessarily large councils of some other West African cities.

Like most of these other cities, its functions are somewhat limited in comparison with municipalities in Britain, since

[1] The Ordinance of 1893 had in fact been preceded by a similar Ordinance in the Gold Coast, which created the municipalities of Cape Coast and Accra in 1858. These, however, were short-lived failures, for in 1861 the Ordinance had to be repealed.

the Government of Sierra Leone retains direct responsibility for certain services which are normally regarded as municipal, for example town-planning, public health and police. Nevertheless, its range of activities gives rise to eight committees, finance and general purposes, municipal trading (principally markets), charity, establishment, health, housing and building, protection, recreational facilities and assessment (of rates); it is also a local education authority. It is divided into seven departments, and employs as principal officers a town clerk, a city treasurer, a town engineer, a water engineer, a chief fire officer, a valuation officer and an education officer in charge of primary education.

Its expenditure is in the neighbourhood of £300,000.

In the rural areas surrounding Freetown, in what used to be known as the Colony, there is a special arrangement which derives from the historical development of the country and the needs of the original immigrant 'creole' population. This is now established under the Rural Areas Ordinance of 1950, and consists of a hierarchy of councils, chosen by indirect election, and comprising village committees, rural district councils and the Rural Areas Council. The work of these committees and councils is usual to rural local authorities anywhere, and the arrangement seems somewhat elaborate for the purpose it serves. A point of interest is that property rating applies throughout the rural area.

Having sketched the system of local government in Sierra Leone in outline, it remains to see what comments or conclusions can be made. Both the principal types of local authority are unusual in their origin; the chiefdom is a projection into modern times of a traditional form of government; its supreme advantage is that it is understood by the mass of the people, for whom it is the natural focus of local loyalty, and in a largely illiterate and unsophisticated population this probably outweighs the disadvantage of trying to do a modern job with a rather old-fashioned tool. The district council is certainly a modern tool, designed for functional purposes, but it has never quite fulfilled the hopes that were placed on it. Moreover, both chiefdoms and districts have to be seen against the background of the province, the decentralized form of government which is being strengthened under the supervision of the Resident Minister, and which commands most of the technical and professional skill available in the country in its own departments.

If we regard provincial administration as the local arm of central government, the question inevitably arises of whether at the 'local' government level there is room for both chiefdom and district. This is an excellent illustration of the problem which faces local government planners everywhere, and in all circumstances. Is the most important consideration to design units which are viable, i.e. can command the financial resources to employ the staff and buy the equipment which will promote tangible development? Or is it more important to have areas to which people are accustomed, and to which they have an inherited sense of belonging? Invariably there is some conflict between the two, and almost invariably planners have to compromise between them. In Sierra Leone this dilemma is very clearly posed. The chiefdoms are necessary because they are all that most people understand; units higher than chiefdoms are necessary, because many of these are little more than native courts and tax-collecting authorities. But is the district council the right answer? That is to say, are the existing groupings of chiefdoms the right ones, or ought they to be larger, bearing in mind the fact that the province necessarily has some of the aspects of a local authority itself? In the largest and least populated Northern Province there are 5 districts, in the South-Western Province 4 and in the South-Eastern Province 3. Since it would not be easy to combine any two districts without making them unmanageable as local authorities, and since the step from the chiefdom to the province would be too great, it is unlikely that any good would come of merely re-drawing the local government map; in which case the way forward might be to devolve more provincial functions on to the districts. However, all we can do in a study of this kind is to ask the questions; only the people on the spot can answer them. We raise them here because they illustrate a fundamental problem of local government.

But the real difficulty in Sierra Leone is that of all the countries we have discussed, namely that resources and skill are too thinly spread. We shall return to the point in the concluding chapter.

Two small but potentially significant points also emerge from this chapter in comparison with previous ones—the right of local Members of Parliament to sit on the district councils (though this is paralleled in Northern Nigeria with the native authorities), and the device of 'assigning' provincial staff to them. The first is unusual, particularly to the British observer, who would find it difficult to imagine his local MP taking a seat as of right in the county council; this might, however, have its advantages. The second is less unusual, and an approach to it is made, for example, in Western Nigeria, where local education officers are posted to the LEAs, which are largely though not wholly conterminous with the local authorities; and where at one time government administrative officers were seconded to act as secretaries to certain local authorities, a practice which is still provided for by statute in Ghana. Here are two further ways in which local government in West Africa has diverged from the 'British model', though Sierra Leone has never been committed to copying this model to the same extent as Southern Nigeria and Ghana.

One disagreeable matter which it is necessary to mention if an objective account of local government in Sierra Leone is to be given is the extremely low standard of financial control and integrity. The Government auditor has the task of auditing the accounts of the districts, the townships and the municipality (it is impossible for him to do so for the chiefdoms) and in every single case, including—regrettably—the Freetown City Council, he has had to report that financial control has been irresponsible. His criticisms admit genuine inefficiency, due to lack of skill and training, but they also make it clear that there is a great deal of dishonesty and peculation. This is a universal problem in West Africa; it may only be that the Government auditor of Sierra Leone is more outspoken than most. Arrears of local tax and property rates have also been at a consistently, and depressingly, high level.

To conclude on a more hopeful note, it is encouraging to see that (as in Nigeria and Ghana) local government, in spite of its many shortcomings, has taken a steadily increasing share of the burden of administration, and in each succeeding year has raised and spent more money for public purposes. The following figures illustrate the point:[1]

Total expenditure by chiefdoms

	£
1939	15,365
1949	139,254
1959	982,882

Expenditure by three selected district councils

	1951 (actual)	1961 (actual)	1962 (estimated)
Council A	8,897	26,310	59,787
Council B	16,581	74,533	98,026
Council C	7,284	63,372	64,920

---

[1] Sierra Leone Protectorate Handbook.

CHAPTER 12

Some Questions for the Future

WE have been describing variations on a theme—the theme of how to share out the work of public administration between central, provincial and local authorities. We have described also how in Southern Nigeria and Ghana an imported institution largely failed, but how it is now beginning to show new life as it puts down roots in native soil.

As to the first, the core of the problem is how to make the best use of resources which are too thinly spread. It was hoped that by giving the new local authorities wider responsibilities than their predecessors departments of central or provincial governments would be relieved of some of their burdens, and would be able to use their resources more profitably for provincial or national purposes; but it has been found that unless local authorities are assigned a very minor role, which they can fulfil with small revenues and unskilled staff, this is no solution to the problem, as the authorities must continue to lean on the Government for financial support and technical aid. Indeed, it is common to find both technical officers and civil servants becoming somewhat impatient with local authorities because of their lack of understanding, or interest, or efficiency in their several fields of work; to achieve their ends through the medium of local government is less satisfactory than to do so direct through their own field organization. Town and country planning, for example, is a matter in which local councils ought to be vitally interested, but Government experts tend to by-pass them in favour of more intelligent and competent bodies created for the special purpose. Agricultural, veterinary and forestry officers also feel they could do better with their own organization than with local bodies more interested in politics than applied science. However, local authorities have built themselves up over ten years into bodies which spend a fair proportion of the public revenue, and which have established their usefulness within a limited range, including a share in education and the main responsibility for sanitation, minor public works, especially local roads and markets, and a number of other local amenities. But do they stop there or do they go on? The original intention was that weight should gradually be shifted from central departments to local authorities, but this can only be done if the local authorities are themselves strong enough to take an increasing burden, and this in turn depends upon their possessing more resources in money and skill than they do at the moment. This is the vicious circle that has to be broken. At the moment the authorities seem to have reached the limit of their usefulness, and the tendency to take back certain services under direct ministerial or departmental control is a symptom of this. In point of time, the reform of native administration took place before the new impetus for development in the 1950's, and the local government laws placed upon local authorities responsibilities which the technical departments, in the light of their growing knowledge, staff and skill would now prefer to administer direct. The problem is made more difficult by the new growth of provincial (or in the Ghanaian sense regional) government, for it poses the unavoidable question of whether there is room for so many different levels of authority. If money and skill were more freely available this would be no problem at all, for the work of local development is limitless. But—to repeat—the core of the problem is how to make the best use of resources which are too thinly spread.

This leads to the second question—was it wise, in Southern Nigeria and Ghana, to import a foreign system? The former British administrations in these countries are sometimes criticized for having imposed their own political institutions, but this criticism hardly stands examination. The local government institutions which the British imposed prior to

1950 were certainly not British; if anything they were French. After 1950 it is true that the Eastern Nigerian Ordinance of 1951 owed much to British officials, who did a good deal of research into the local government institutions of their own country, though one of them was sent to study local government in Kenya and Uganda in preparation for the new Ordinance;[1] and this Ordinance, perhaps unfortunately, was later widely copied in Ghana and Western Nigeria. But in Ghana the reform of the native authorities was the sole responsibility of a committee of Ghanaians,[2] which said

". . . we have attempted, in effect, to achieve a synthesis of the traditional type of local government in this country with the more developed democratic form of local government in the United Kingdom, which, after careful consideration, we have taken as our model *rather than that of either France or America.*' (Author's italics.)

In Western Nigeria the British Administration, by now alerted to the danger of planting a foreign institution in Nigerian soil, did its best to persuade the Government not to copy British local government, but to continue with the policy of gradualism, by which young and educated men were being 'infiltrated' into the traditional native authorities; it failed, as its warnings aroused suspicion that the imperialists were trying to put them off with something that was second best. Nigerians were as insistent on the British model of local government as on the Westminster model of Parliament. The carbon copy—the phrase is hardly an exaggeration —failed for reasons which we have discussed in earlier chapters. The amendments which were made to the earlier laws have improved the position, but only up to a point, and we are left with the large question of what is likely to be the most useful line of future development. The answer to this question turns on the two inseparable factors of control and structure.

[1] *African Local Government Reform—Kenya, Uganda and Eastern Nigeria:* by Brigadier E. J. Gibbons, 1949.
[2] Report of the Committee on Constitutional Reform, presided over by the late Sir Henly Coussey, 1949.

In all the countries we are considering it is assumed that control should be in the hands of elected councillors. But are these in fact the most appropriate people? In the short run, obviously not, for their record, taking them as a whole, condemns them out of hand. Perhaps the most conclusive evidence for this is that when, as has frequently happened, a council has been dissolved and a 'committee of management' has taken its place, this committee has provided more efficient, economical and honest service than its elected predecessors. This 'caretaker' committee has been chosen, by nomination, from people who have proved themselves to be competent in various walks of life, and these, alas, are the very people who are not normally to be found on local councils. The successful trader or professional man, who ought to be prominent in local government, would not normally face the rigours of a local government election, nor would he be invited to do so unless he were deep in party politics. In Western Nigeria there is an even sadder comment on local representative democracy, for the Government now favours not a caretaker committee but a 'sole administrator', armed with the powers and prestige of a colonial administrator of long ago. One such sole administrator, in the important town of Abeokuta, placed local administration, including local tax collecting, on a firmer basis than it had been for many years, and gave great satisfaction to the people in doing so. All this is not to condemn local democracy, but to question whether the material for local democracy exists at the present time.

Curiously enough, there is ample evidence that local democracy does work very well indeed, especially at the village level, but only if left alone, and not if 'institutionalized' in the laws. In Eastern Nigeria especially, the innumerable 'clan unions' represent local democracy at its best, in the sense that people raise large sums of money without difficulty and spend them without dishonesty or waste on scholarships, village improvements and the care of those in need. There is wide agreement that these unions are often more effective than the statutory local authorities, though they have no legal existence, receive no grant aid from the Government and have no power to levy rates compulsorily. They do not need this last power, however, because people pay their dues without compulsion, for if they failed to do so they would offend against the unwritten laws of their community, which are more potent than the written laws of the State. Loyalty to the union has its own compulsive power, whereas the statutory local council has as yet no place in the affections of the people.

Indigenous institutions, especially when they have a 'clannish' or 'tribal' basis, cannot survive indefinitely, at any rate in their original form, in a world of party politics, public corporations and industrialization, but at the present time there is no denying that their authority is more powerful than that of the local councils.

It is of course one of the difficulties of government in societies which are in such rapid transition that the organs of modern administration are alien, so far as most people's real affections are concerned, and that even their own elected parliaments and governments are distant and incomprehensible bodies. One of the purposes which local government could serve would be to bridge this gulf, since an elected councillor on the doorstep is more understandable than an elected Member of Parliament in a distant capital.

A good deal turns, however, on what the councillors are expected to do. It is one thing for elected representatives to be 'associated' with the government of their locality, but quite another for them to control it in detail; there are naturally degrees in between, and the problem in West Africa is really that of finding the right degree. Many people have thought in recent years that a balance more suitable to West African conditions between the authority of the civil service, the local government staff and the elected councillor has been struck in Eire than in Britain, and that if West Africa must have a 'model' the Irish model would be a better one than the British. In the context of this book Irish local government deserves a brief digression.

Ireland was governed as part of the United Kingdom until

1922, with the full apparatus of British central and local government controlled from Whitehall. In 1922 it became a 'Free State' within the British Commonwealth, in the manner of a free dominion; in 1937 it became an independent country in the manner later followed by Ghana, i.e. with a presidential form of government, linked to the Commonwealth only through recognition of the Monarch as the head of the 'family'; in 1949 it became a fully independent Republic. These developments had their consequences for local government.

From 1922 onwards the British form of local government started to suffer a decline. Corruption and inefficiency were both contributory factors, but the more fundamental fact was that the system was unsuitable for Ireland. The British system had evolved in a wealthy country and at a time when revenues were buoyant, for it is not a cheap form of government; Ireland by contrast was a poor country. Britain was industrial and urban, but with a prosperous rural population of middle-class country dwellers and large-scale farmers; Ireland was predominantly a country of small—indeed to a large extent peasant subsistence—farmers. Britain could therefore draw on a considerable class of prosperous people who were public spirited and to whom local government was a hobby; Ireland could not. Communications in Britain were good, so that councillors could travel easily and quickly to their innumerable committee meetings; this was not so in Ireland.

Accordingly, independent Ireland set about devising its own system of local government based on county and city 'managers', which took shape as early as 1928 and was consolidated in the County Management Acts of 1940 and 1942. This system was essentially a compromise between a number of other systems, and a student of comparative local government could find in it elements of British, French and American origin. The essential fact is that it suited the circumstances of Ireland. What emerged from these Acts was a difference of emphasis between the respective responsibilities of the manager and the council, as compared with those of the English clerk and council. The method of appointing the manager was significant, for this was not left to the free choice of the council; the manager was appointed by the Minister of Local Government, acting on the recommendation of the 'Local Appointments Commissioners' (a kind of Local Government Service Board), who would normally recommend, if they were candidates, an existing county secretary or secretary to a board of health; thus the appointment was ministerially controlled. The manager, once appointed, assumed a much larger degree of executive responsibility than his British counterpart, though not as much as his counterpart—the city manager—in many American cities, whose role is closer to that of the managing director of a business firm *vis-à-vis* his board of directors.

This did not, however, mean that the function of the elected councils was ornamental, or that their powers were negligible. On the contrary all the *essential* powers of democratic local government were specifically reserved to them in a Schedule of the 1940 Act; they included, notably, the power to make a rate, to borrow money, to make, amend or revoke a by-law, to award scholarships, and to make certain decisions under the Town and Regional Planning and the Housing Acts. What it did mean, however, in practice, was that the county councils confined themselves to decisions of policy on these major matters, but did not hold such frequent meetings, nor break up into such an elaborate network of committees, as their British counterparts, for the purpose of supervising in detail the way in which policy was implemented. This was not necessarily less democratic than British practice, which indeed involves some very curious paradoxes, since some committees and sub-committees are apt to lose themselves in discussion of very minor details which should be decided by officials, while leaving officials a remarkable amount of freedom in major matters of policy; or again they will haggle over the expenditure of a few pounds on some item which happens to have caught their attention, and then pass the expenditure of hundreds of thousands without a second thought. The Irish county councils had of course full supervisory powers and in an extremity they could, by a two-thirds majority, suspend a manager and, with the Minister's consent, remove him; there was thus no doubt that the council was the controlling power. The difference of emphasis lay in the way in which local government is tackled as a problem in *management*.

These arrangements were amended by the Local Government (County Administration) Act of 1950, which again altered the balance of authority between the professional administrator and the elected representative. The functions of the county councils were recast into three categories—the 'scheduled' functions to which we have already referred; 'employment, tenancy and personal health functions' which were to be performed by the county manager; and a number of other, so-called 'executive', functions, previously performed by the manager, which were now to be performed by two statutory executive committees of the council; one a 'general executive committee', dealing primarily with contracts, construction and maintenance; the other a 'health executive committee' dealing with wider questions of public health than those left within the discretion of the manager. Incidentally, the 'county manager' was re-styled the 'county officer' and his post amalgamated with that of the county secretary.

Although this represented a 'swing of the pendulum' back to British ideas, the diffusion of responsibility and the proliferation of committees was still less than in Britain and the independence of the chief officer greater. But, most significantly, the manager system saw Ireland through the first generation of political independence, when the withdrawal of British controlled officials had left the local authorities in an awkward stage of transition.

The similarities between the historical development of local government in Ireland and West Africa are too striking to need emphasis, and although any outward similarities between the two countries have long since disappeared, the experience of Ireland is likely to be more relevant to West Africa than that of Britain. It is certainly the view of experienced people that West African local government as it is today involves too many councillors, too many committees and too much interference in the realm of management. The county management system applies, with slight modifications, in the four or five principal cities of Ireland, and the idea of city managers has aroused even more interest in West Africa than that of managers for rural areas.

Here, then, is one possible development in the future of control. There are many others. At the opposite extreme, for example, there is control by the 'executive councillors' in Northern Nigeria; it is perhaps a little strange that the policy of the Northern Government is aimed at gradually transferring the powers of these councillors to committees; this would conform to fashion, but there is no inherent reason why this 'Cabinet' form of local government should not serve the needs of the larger and wealthier emirates better than either managers or committees, unless or until the electors show unmistakably that they are opposed to it; it is, after all, a type of government which finds some support in Britain in relation to big cities and heavily populated and industrial counties.

What is necessary above all is to preserve an open mind, to refuse to be influenced unduly by the practice of other countries where circumstances are wholly different, and to settle on a system of control which will, in *local* circumstances, satisfy as far as possible two needs which are always apt to be in conflict with one another—representative control on the one hand and managerial efficiency on the other. It is one of the dilemmas of democracy that the two do not always coincide, and that a compromise has to be devised between them.

We have spoken of control; it is now necessary to say something about structure.

A fact which soon becomes apparent in West Africa is that governments have not made up their minds about the purpose of decentralization; so that different, and sometimes opposing, policies appear to be followed at the same time.

Broadly speaking, local government in West Africa has two aims—the development of social and technical services, and the association with this development of the elected representatives of the people in local areas. Again, the two aims are not necessarily compatible, and again it may be necessary to compromise between them. Looking at the question purely from a government's point of view, with development as the principal aim, there are four possibilities. They may regard local authorities as the channel through which all development will take place, in which case the authorities would need to be very much bigger than they are; they may undertake all development themselves through their ministries and technical departments, in which case the local authorities will be left with only minor duties of sanitation and markets; they may attempt some kind of partnership with the local authorities, involving subsidies of money and staff; or they may make a clear-cut division between their own functions and those of local authorities. Traces of all four, and occasionally mixtures of all four, may be found in Nigeria, Ghana and Sierra Leone today.

But leaving aside these questions of long-term policy, we may agree that with the exception of the Northern 'emirate-NAS' the typical local authorities are not large enough in area, population or finance to contribute to development in other than minor ways. This is largely because they were built on the foundation of the indigenous native authorities, and these were too small for the development age. There is an interesting contrast here with parts of East Africa, and especially with Kenya. Local government in Kenya was not built upon indigenous authorities, because there were none, or at least they were too fragmented and primitive to offer a firm foundation. Accordingly, as the need for local government became apparent the Government, as far back as 1924, devised new areas, which were based primarily upon administrative convenience and secondarily upon tribal solidarity. These developed over forty years into the African district councils of today, by a gradual process of devolving responsibility upon them and freeing them from the supervision of the district commissioners. By the time they reached some measure of independence they had the great advantage of being 'viable' in size, or in plain language of being big enough to be effective for the purposes of modern development. Accordingly, those in the central and heavily populated areas of the country budget for revenues of between a quarter and half a million pounds instead of £40–50,000; they are able to employ expatriate staff, especially in their treasuries, and the Government of Kenya is able to associate them in varying degrees with national development plans. In Uganda the position is comparable, though for a mixture of reasons; in some parts indigenous institutions provided the foundation, but these were integrated 'kingdoms' of considerable size; in others the administrative districts were carved out on a bolder pattern.

Faced with this problem of small authorities, the West African governments seem to have two alternatives; either to proceed on the assumption that local authorities are to be part of the apparatus of national development, in which case they must become bigger; or on the assumption that local government is strictly *local* and concerned with the affairs of the 'parish pump', and that the agencies for development must be the new provincial and regional authorities which have established themselves everywhere except in Western Nigeria. Western Nigeria is in fact, at the moment of writing, something of a test case, since for various reasons it has not yet committed itself to any radical departure from its British origins, while on the other hand more radical thinking has been done about the future than anywhere else—thinking in which the creation of viable authorities for particular purposes, the Irish managerial system and the parallel existence of modern and traditional bodies have all played their part.

If it is agreed that, for whatever reason, local authorities must combine in order to be bigger, there are only two possible ways of bringing it about; one is by compulsion and the other by persuasion. Compulsion, in a matter of this kind, usually defeats itself. Both local loyalties and political passions become roused, opposition becomes organized, and any possibility of constructive work disappears in an atmosphere of ill-will and misunderstanding. Local government is essentially team-work in which the personal factor counts for a great deal, and enemies cannot be forced to be friends. Persuasion has never been tried, though an interesting possibility was suggested by the Commissioner for Local Government Enquiries for Ghana in 1957.[1] Dealing with this very problem, he suggested to his Government that one alternative might be for the main local government services —public works, roads, education, police, water supplies, clinics and dispensaries—to rest in principle with the regional authorities, as being the ones most obviously capable of administering them, leaving the minor services to the small local councils which existed at the time. He suggested, however, that the regional authorities should be able to delegate their powers to local authorities according to their populations; for example, those with over 50,000 population would qualify to administer local roads, primary and middle education, clinics and dispensaries and water schemes; those with 30,000 (or in the case of urban councils 20,000) primary education, clinics and dispensaries and local water supplies; and those with 20,000 primary education and local water supplies. He added 'It might encourage amalgamations of local councils if they knew that by doing so they could operate larger powers. Attendance allowances to councillors would be graded according to the extent of the powers which the council operates.' The latter sentence appears to hover on the border-line between persuasion and bribery! The more serious point, however, is that the plan offered a method of legitimate persuasion. Local councils would be told that if they wished to stay as they were no one would try to stop them, and they could continue to look after markets, sanitation and lorry parks; but if they chose to combine they could acquire these wider responsibilities.

This plan was in fact rejected by the Government in favour

[1] See footnote to p. 19. The reduction in the number of councils in Ghana from 278 to 69 was, of course, a fairly successful example of compulsion.

of the alternative, which aimed at creating throughout the country a medium-sized multi-purpose authority, so we shall never know how the local councils would have responded to the opportunity—or temptation. But it throws an interesting idea into the general pool.

It is not, of course, necessary to equate local government with 'development'; much depends on how this word is defined. If we think of it in terms of 'infra-structure', that is main roads, railways, telecommunications, research centres, hospitals and industrialization, then local government is obviously not concerned with these. Traditionally, or at any rate in the British tradition, local government has been concerned with social services rather than development, although it is not possible to draw an altogether firm distinction between the two; for example, education and health are part of the infra-structure of national development, and local government is concerned with both, even though in West Africa its share is largely restricted to primary education and local sanitary services. But even the relatively modest work of local government as it stands requires units of a minimum size. We mentioned on p. 86 that the Government of Western Nigeria had done some investigation into the optimum areas in which to administer education and public health, and a recent United Nations publication[1] has carried out some similar research dealing with rural educational, health, agricultural and personal social services. The point is that there *are* these objective standards by which the proper size for local authorities can be measured. They must then be balanced against the size which is acceptable to public opinion because of traditional loyalties, and in West Africa, apart from the emirates, this generally turns out to be very much smaller. In making the final decision more attention has generally been paid to the second criterion than the first, and the tendency has been to settle down to the small–medium type of area ('county' in Eastern Nigeria, 'district'

[1] Decentralization for National and Local Development: United Nations Technical Assistance Programme.

in Western Nigeria, 'local' in Ghana and 'district' in Sierra Leone) which makes the best—or possibly the worst?—of both worlds.

This is seen very clearly in Western Nigeria, where there is still a three-tier structure of divisional, district and local councils, but where it is slowly disintegrating. The divisional council is the largest unit, and has some traditional sanction both ethnically and because it was the effective area of colonial administration, to which people had become accustomed during half a century. But 'Divisional councils are unpopular and are gradually dying out. It would appear that old ties are weakening... Government servants deplore the disappearance of the divisional councils because they are the only units large enough to provide efficient organization for such services as education, public works and public health. There is a groping towards "service authorities" which will cover similar areas but which will avoid the political odium which divisional councils have earned.'[1] At the other end of the scale the 'local' councils are too small for effective administration, save in the most minor matters, and the Government itself has allowed many of them to lapse simply by withholding the financial support that was necessary to keep them going; they have faded away into so-called 'area committees', which are little more than a very local forum for local public opinion.

Are the twin aims of local government—getting things done and getting them done under local representative control—incompatible in West Africa today? Ought we to regard local government simply in terms of the most effective method of decentralization instead of an exercise in democracy?

There is little doubt that the rush towards democracy in local government was too precipitate, because it resulted in the opposite of democracy. There is always a level of under-

---

[1] Chief J. M. Beckley, Permanent Secretary, Ministry of Local Government, Western Nigeria, quoted in the foregoing United Nations document.

standing below which democracy has no meaning, because instead of the people exercising power they are manipulated by a few people who exercise it in their name; in many of the local councils in West Africa neither electors nor elected had any clear picture of what local government was about, and this has resulted in its absorption into party machines, its fragmentation for local political reasons, and its exploitation through systematic bribery and corruption. Above all it has failed to attract the only people who could be expected to make it work—the business and professional community, the educated middle class in general, and those who had shown by their achievement in any walk of life that they had earned the right to be leaders in their locality in terms of the modern, rather than the traditional, world. In the long run it may not greatly matter that this has happened, but the aim of policy must obviously be to see that it does not happen again.

The new provincial or regional groupings, or the new 'service authorities' towards which Western Nigeria is said to be groping, have an opportunity to avoid the mistakes of the past, by making the qualifications for elected persons higher, by restricting them to their proper field of policy making and keeping them out of administration (or alternatively, as in Northern Nigeria, placing responsibility for administration firmly upon them, so that they have to answer for their own shortcomings), and by removing altogether the possibility of personal enrichment. Democracy becomes more meaningful as people become more educated, and the mere passage of time will no doubt remove some of the worst abuses. Meanwhile, there is no reason why governments, by exercising firm control themselves, should not prevent the people from being exploited in the name of democracy.

The Northern emirates rarely fit into this discussion, and they have their own peculiar interest. Their advantages are obvious, though recent enquiries into some of them, notably the monolithic Kano NA, have revealed that all is not well under the surface, and that corruption and maladministration are as great a danger there as anywhere else. Their policy of more gradual change, instead of a plunge into the unknown, seems to have been wise, and over most of the Region there is little evidence that the mass of people, however poor they may be, are discontented or are demanding radical change in the native authorities. But this is a dangerous thing to say in the 1960's, and much will depend on whether change is so gradual as to amount to complacency. There are very few people living in 1950 who can claim to have foreseen with any accuracy that the apparently well-established British colonial régime in West Africa would have disappeared by 1960, and this applies to Briton and African alike. It is possible, by analogy, that below the surface steadiness, patience and fatalism of Islam there is a greater striving for rapid change towards a more representative democracy than is generally supposed.

Meanwhile, however, the amount of change that has already taken place must not be underrated, and the emirates appear to be the most successful examples of local government in combining effectiveness with representative growth.

In conclusion, we revert to the 'British model'. Looking back with the advantage of hindsight, it is remarkable what a parochial view was taken of the possible ways in which the old native authorities could be modernized, or in which a more effective system of local government put in their place. Why should it be supposed that the local government of part of a small island off the north coast of Europe, steeped in its own history and tradition, should have any relevance to the situation in developing Africa? Since the late 1940's many fresh windows have been opened on Africa, experts have poured in from countries with whom West Africa previously had little or no contact, bringing wholly new ideas, and Africans themselves have studied developments in Asia, Israel, Latin America and other countries whose problems are more closely related to their own. In the more academic realm, investigations and comparative research into local administration have covered the world. The recent United Nations Report to which reference has been made studies 'patterns in decentralization' in such varied countries as Brazil, France, India, Poland, Senegal, Sudan, the United Arab Republic, the United Kingdom, the United States of America, Western Nigeria and Yugoslavia. Such studies were lacking in 1945-50, when plans for reorganizing local government in West Africa were taking shape, and Britain was taken as the yardstick partly because administrators were British and partly because in those days 'British was best' even in the minds of the Africans who were seeking to throw off British colonial government. Both parties to the contract were equally guilty of parochialism.

It is, however, natural that the institutions of a country which had been the ruling power for sixty years or more should have made their influence felt, and in spite of disappointments and mistakes a good deal has been achieved. At a recent ECA Seminar on 'Urgent Administrative Problems of African Governments' at Addis Ababa the assembled senior civil servants, all African, and representing nearly all the former British and French colonial territories, agreed that the pioneering work of the colonial powers in introducing local government had been well worth while, and that the future by no means called for a reversal of policy but only for a greater adaptation to local conditions.

It may not be inappropriate, therefore, to end this book with an appreciation of how the development of local government in the African colonies appeared through British eyes.

In the decade which followed the Second World War the Colonial Office developed more positive social policies in Africa than at any time in its history. Under the post-war Labour Government's second colonial secretary, Mr Arthur Creech Jones, there was a remarkable shift in emphasis in the matters with which the Office concerned itself. The shift was towards such things as trade unions, co-operatives and 'representative and efficient local government'.

Today, nearly twenty years later, the colonial empire in

Africa belongs to the past, welfare policies are taken for granted, and the Labour Government's achievements now seem modest when set against the massive international aid and expertise that has since been concentrated in Africa. Indeed, some of their policies now seem somewhat naïve, and few of their achievements have justified what we now see to have been a somewhat simple faith in the perfectibility of the masses, inspired by the history of the British working class. It is necessary to understand how the problem looked to the British Government in 1945, before the international searchlights had been turned on Africa.

There is little doubt from the official records of the first half of this century that the British Government had always supposed that the West African colonies would some day be self-governing; there is equally little doubt that few pre-war Colonial Office officials or Colonial Governors imagined that this would happen in their own lifetime. Even the postwar Gold Coast Government did not take the point even when a revolution was developing under their noses. The Colonial Office, on the other hand, was increasingly aware in the late 1940's not only that the inevitable tide of self-government was approaching the flood, but that the West African colonies were ill-prepared for its consequences. The critics of the Labour Government who accused them of unnaturally stimulating the approach of self-government had got their facts the wrong way round. The Government knew what was coming, knew that the colonies were unprepared for it, and set about preparing some emergency tidal defences; for the Labour Party had sufficient sense of history to know that the revolutionary nationalism of the underprivileged nations needed no stimulus, and that it was irresistible. This was the sole advantage they had over their predecessors and political opponents, whose knowledge, experience and interest in colonial matters was otherwise infinitely greater, but whose political instincts kept them out of touch with the deeper realities.

The pressure on colonial governments to develop trade unions, co-operatives and local government derived from a truer instinct. In actual execution the policy went astray in almost every particular, as they accepted too easily the idea that a social institution could be exported, and that what was known to be good for the British working man must inevitably be good for his African counterpart; but the policy itself was sensitive, and by the standards of twenty years ago far-sighted; for in these twenty years there has been concentrated a revolution of thought and understanding about Africa that would in pre-war days have occupied a century. In such matters, more than most, it would be unreasonable to judge the actions of one generation in the light of the intellectual and moral standards of the next.

Trade unions, it was argued, would prepare the growing wage-earning class for responsible negotiation and industrial democracy, and their involvement in local and international rivalries before they had any achievement to their credit were not foreseen, nor was the shallowness of their roots properly appreciated. Co-operatives would prepare the farmers for rural democracy by encouraging self-help in providing credits, tools, seeds and marketing arrangements; they have had some success, though their democracy has been subject to more guidance than the co-operative enthusiasts had hoped. Local government would prepare all sections of the community for the responsibilities of independence, especially—in accordance with a theory particularly dear to the British—by acting as a local training school for eventual parliamentarians and ministers. This worthy but unimaginative aim found little response among the articulate nationalists, who were only concerned with political independence and with power in the central government; and in many parts of West Africa local government has promoted more problems than it has solved.

This book has been an attempt to examine an activity which absorbed an extraordinarily high proportion of the energies of West African governments between 1950 and 1960, which has some value as a case study in comparative administration, which has had many failures and disappointments, but which has on the other hand been entirely necessary. For although administrators and anthropologists alike have criticized what has been done, few critics have maintained that what preceded it was better, or have been able to say with confidence how the swift transition from a local tribal parliament to a modern-type local authority could have been more adroitly guided, given the undoubted need and the irresistible demand for the latter.

INDEX

Administrative officers (colonial), 11
Administrative officers (contemporary), 103–5
Aldermen, 42
Audit, 101, 161

'British model', 10, 164, 178
By-laws, 77, 148
   'Rules' (N. Nigeria), 137–8

Chiefs, 11, 37, 147
Civil Servants in local government, 48, 154–5
'Commissioners' (Ministerial or political), 105–6, 144, 145
Committees, 35, 131, 171
Contracts, 79
'Conventions' 36, 43, 51, 60
Councillors
   general, 13, 25 et seq., 166–7, 171
   duties of, 32
   relationship to staff, 43–5, 150
   remuneration of, 27
   special position in N. Nigeria 130
Courts, local, 77, 148

Decentralisation and devolution, 11 n., 163, 171–2
Default powers, 97
Delegated legislation, 97
District Councils (Sierra Leone) 152–4

Education, 19 n., 55, 68, 70

Fees, 121–2
Freetown, 158

Grants, 9–13, 140

Housing, 69, 92

Inspection, 96, 102, 105
Instruments, 15, 16

Joint Boards & Committees, 88

Kano Native Authority, 127, 177

Lagos, 93
Loans, 123–4
Licences, 122–3
Local authorities
   as agents of Government, 61, 96, 99
   and national standards, 97
   functions of, 19, 67 et seq., 135–8, 150, 155–7
   nomenclature of
      British, 15, 23–4
      West African, 15, 125, 145
   relationship with central government, 96 et seq., 164
   size and structure
      British, 13, 18, 82–4
      West Africa, 18, 20, 85–88, 138–9, 160, 171–5
Local government (other systems)
   in France, 11–12
   in the U.S.A., 12
   in Eire, 167–70

M.P's on local councils, 135, 154, 161
Minister, powers of, 99–101

Native authorities, 11, 18, 37

Outer Councils (N. Nigeria), 135

Parliament, comparison with, 37, 65, 131

Party politics, 51, 57 et seq.
  Sardauna of Sokoto, statement by, 62
Police forces (local), 68, 76
Political control—see 'Commissioners'
Precepts, 82, 150
Provincial government (N. Nigeria), 142-3

Rates, 113-20
  N. Nigeria & Sierra Leone—see Tax
Registration of births and deaths, 73, 149

'Sons of the soil', 46
Staffs of local authorities
  general, 13, 41 et seq.
  duties of, 52
  relationship to central government, 45-9
  relationship to councillors, 43-5, 50
Subordinate authorities (N. Nigeria), 131-4
Surcharge, 30, 101

Tax, 139 (N. Nigeria), 151 (Sierra Leone)
Technical skills, 54-5
'Tiers', 16, 18, 20
Town planning, 91
Towns, 15, 21-3, 31, 90-1, 93, 141, 157-9
Traditional members, 33, 37-40

Ultra vires, 75, 101, 155
Unified local government service, 45-8

For Product Safety Concerns and Information please contact our EU
representative GPSR@taylorandfrancis.com
Taylor & Francis Verlag GmbH, Kaufingerstraße 24, 80331 München, Germany

www.ingramcontent.com/pod-product-compliance
Lightning Source LLC
Chambersburg PA
CBHW061448300426
44114CB00014B/1889